They Are

Trying Anymore:

The A's, B's, and DD's of Getting Older

An Alphabet of Essays About Aging

Hollie Grimaldi-Flores

Copyright © 2024 by Hollie Grimaldi-Flores

All Rights Reserved. No part of this publication may be reproduced, stored in a retrieval system, or transmitted in any form or by any means (electronic, mechanical, photocopying, recording, or otherwise) without the written permission of the author.

Library of Congress Control Number:
2024914075

Tin Cat Media
Nevada City, California

Paperback ISBN#: 978-0-9826723-8-9
eBook ISBN#: 978-0-9826723-9-6

Book Cover original sketch by Tea Wade
Formatting and Design by Jenaii Sabanal and Shanin Martin, Immersion Marketing

Dedication

For those who have always believed I could write a book.

Contents

	Introduction	vii
1	"A" is for Aging	1
2	"B" is for Breasts	7
3	"C" is for Change	13
4	"D" is for Death	17
5	"E" is for Exercise	23
6	"F" is for Forgetful	27
7	"G" is for Gratitude	31
8	"H" is for Hot (Flash)	37
9	"I" is for Intimacy	41
10	"J" is for Joy	45
11	"K" is for Kids	49
12	"L" is for Laughter	55
13	"M" is for Many (including Menopause)	59
14	"N" is for Neck	63

15	"O" is for Old	69
16	"P" is for Pain	77
17	"Q" is for Quinquagenarian	81
18	"R" is for Relative	85
19	"S" is for Sleep	91
20	"T" is for Technology	95
21	"U" is for Un	101
22	"V" is for Vision	105
23	"W" is for Weary	109
24	"X" is for Xerosis	115
25	"Y" is for Youth	121
26	"Z" is for Zig Zag	125
	Acknowledgements	
	About the Author	

Introduction

It may have been my therapist who first said, "You should write a book." I have heard it many times since, but you must think when your therapist says so maybe there is something there.

I have had a colorful life. I am the youngest of seven children who grew up in extreme poverty until my mother remarried when I was ten and I was catapulted into life in middle class America. While we now had running water, the move came with many unforeseen challenges that set me on a rocky path. There is a book in there, for sure.

But try as I might, I could not get myself to take on the arduous task. All around me, people were writing books, but I couldn't seem to do it.

After many months of trying to write my memoir, including two rounds of a writing class with a successful author, I have 20 solid pages—a look at a decade I spent in a relationship with a bipolar professional roadie set in the backdrop of the 1980's music business. That relationship included marriage, two children and divorce. Most of it was ugly, except the children who are a dream. I decided there are still too many living souls around to tell that tale, so not just yet on that one.

My second husband came with five boys of his own so he would like me to write about our life raising a blended family and all the highs and lows that came with it. He even has a title: "Table for Nine". I am not ready.

On my 60th birthday I was assessing my physique and as my eyes wandered to my drooping breasts a thought came into my head. "It's like they aren't even trying anymore," I surmised. I felt abandoned by my body. Clearly, it was giving up! I was on the brink of a new decade and things were going downhill. Suddenly, the idea for this book took form.

Since 2015, I have been writing a column for my local newspaper. Many people have suggested I turn some of those compositions into an anthology, and I might get there. A few of the following essays have been previously published in some form in that column, so it seemed like a good place to start.

I hope these essays, all covering some aspect of what it is like for a woman in the United States to age, resonate with you on some level and that you are left with a smile, some insight, or simply feeling a little less alone.

"A" is for Aging

As Mae West reputedly said, "Aging is not for the faint of heart." I often add, "But it certainly beats the alternative." This getting older thing has many plusses, though it is the negatives that seem to garner much of the attention, so let me start there.

I am inching ever closer to the age of retirement and with each passing year, I find myself apologizing over and over to my elders who passed this way before me. I'm sorry for the snarky thoughts I had when I would hear them moan or creak or wince when rising from a chair or bending to pick up a dropped item from the floor, or simply walking to the car. "Oh, my aching back" could have been on a t-shirt for the many times I heard my father complain after a long day working (or philandering). He was an auto mechanic and spent many hours crawling underneath or bent over the hood of a car. He was also a womanizer and spent nearly as many hours crawling underneath or bent over a woman, so there is that.

Just like a vehicle with a warranty that expires at 60,000 miles, the human body begins to sputter around the seventh decade. For some sooner, but for me, turning 60 felt like the beginning of a series of breakdowns. My transmission began slipping, getting out of first gear and into a cruising speed required a concerted effort.

Mind you I am still weathering menopause, that passage of hot flashing, hormonally out of balance, hair thinning, skin drying, sleep-depriving storm that began somewhere in my 40's and plagues me to this day. If only that could be remedied with a new air filter and an oil change.

In my youth I was a fearless, reckless, unpredictable woman in motion. I abused my body with considerable portions of alcohol, drugs, carbohydrates, and other bad decisions, but recovery was swift, and any self- inflicted pain passed quickly. I thought myself to be bullet proof.

I never actually got into a regular exercise regimen. Over the course of my life, I have joined several gyms, tried my hand at running, and spent some time enduring both water and land aerobics. For a time, I found swimming to be something I could use to drop some weight and tone my muscles, but it didn't last. I thought maybe I just needed a tune up.

My most recent experience with organized exercise was several years ago when a friend and I would religiously show up for circuit training classes several mornings each week. We became very strong, but we never lost any weight, so we quit the class and started walking together instead. We walked a little over three miles almost every morning. Our legs were strong. Our hearts, likely, appreciated it also, but it did not come without maladies.

Early on I began suffering. The bottom of my feet hurt. What? Was walking going to be a problem? Turns out I had a little something called Planter Fasciitis, which is incredibly painful and caused by inflammation of the thick band of tissue that connects the heel bone to the toes. It made me so mad. I must be able to walk! I refused to quit and sought treatment. Maybe I just needed a better set of tires. Once I found the correct footwear and added ibuprofen as a food group, I was back outside.

Walking helps keep me strong but does nothing to help my arm strength or with general flexibility. I have been trying to talk myself into yoga for a decade. I know it will be good for me. I just don't know how to make myself do it.

I went to what I thought was a beginner's class once. The lady next to me, clearly a couple of decades older, said hello to me and then bent in half. So much for the beginner class! She looked like a life-sized jackknife with her nose touching her knees and her fingers grasping her feet. Now that is flexible.

I attempted the same pose. My body simply refused. My shape was less jackknife and more sickle. My face and knees were barely in the same zip code and my fingertips were so far from my toes that I needed my glasses to clearly see the distance. I did not find it relaxing or empowering. I found it intimidating.

Maybe yoga at home would be the key to success, without menacing pretzel people next to me or worse, someone in "cat pose" staring directly at my back end.

It is obvious that I have a long way to go. As I age, I do understand the importance of a good diet, regular exercise of any kind, and a positive mindset. It might be considered regular maintenance.

I do want to, hope to, and expect to, live for several more decades. The quality of those decades is, in part, up to me.

For certain, genetics can wreak their own brand of havoc. My family DNA comes with high cholesterol, a little heart disease, some diabetes and is no stranger to dementia. I could spend my time focusing on what is out of my control, but instead I am choosing to take the best approach to offset the predisposed issues with what is within my power.

It took years for me to understand that while my high cholesterol may not have been caused as a direct result of any of my own dietary abuses, but rather by my genetic makeup, I still needed to take medication to lower the bad number and keep my arteries open. In other words, it does not matter that it is inherited rather than self-induced. I have it. Medication could help it. I should take the medicine. I only emphasize this point because I spent years resisting the inevitable. I refused to take the little pill because I did not think it was my fault. Why was I being punished? I looked at nonwestern medicinal alternatives, but it all came down to ingesting something to offset the numbers, so I surrendered. I take the pill.

I also caved and reduced the amount of red meat in my diet which promises to push heart disease a little further down the road. My weight plays a factor in diabetes risk, so I continue to track my daily intake and try to make better choices each day. I am certainly a work in progress with the beauty of each new day being an opportunity to do better than the day before.

I blame, make that, attribute, the aforementioned issues to my paternal lineage, but dementia is prominent on my mother's side of the gene pool. And dementia is what it is. I do word puzzles, stay active, read up on best practices, when I remember to do so.

I can control my attitude, my diet and how I treat this vessel. I can commit to stretching, strengthening, and taking myself out for a bike ride or a walk.

If I am "over the hill", shouldn't I be able to cruise through these next few decades? Based on recent experiences, this will not be the case. As with any piece of machinery (and make no mistake, our bodies are very machine-like) regular maintenance is required. And, while I have not completely stalled out, I am clearly due for a tune up, if I intend to keep this motor operating like a high performance vehicle.

My goal is to have a strong mind, a strong body, and a strong soul. It is no easy thing—to take a sedentary lifestyle and shift into a conscious, self-aware, regimented existence, but it is the only way I can see qualifying for the extended warranty. I'm willing to give it a shot.

I realize I have touched on a number of maladies here but think of it as an overview of sorts of what is to come in these next chapters. There may be no winning the race, but I am hoping for many, many more laps around the sun.

Hollie Grimaldi-Flores

"B" is for Breasts

As the youngest of seven children, with a five-year gap between the sixth child and me, I grew up always trying to catch up to my older siblings, in every possible way. I hurried my way through childhood. My mom would tell the story of finding me crawling up onto the toilet at 18 months old as I potty trained myself. I begged my eldest sister to teach me to read before I began kindergarten.

As I grew older, I pleaded with my siblings to include me in every activity. Psychologically, I now understand my need to be perceived as good and pleasant and my need to be liked, came from being included in the lives of my siblings. Being good and pleasant was the only way to get the older siblings to include me or let me tag along. It was how I learned to be accepted.

And phrases like you are too young or too small became an "I'll show you" challenge.

Because of the age disparity, by the time I was five, my older sisters were well into puberty, so it's no wonder that I began praying for breasts before I was in double digits. My siblings teased my boyish figure endlessly. I remember lying on my bed, pulling on my flat chest, begging the good Lord to give me breasts. Please, God! And in a classic case of "be careful what you ask for..." the Lord did deliver. The summer between grade school and junior high my boyish figure transformed into one that was round and curvy—from my "bubble butt" to my larger-than-any-of-my-friends-breasts—I had blossomed.

A popular advice columnist, Ann Landers, once responded to a girl asking how she would know when it was time to wear a bra with a pencil test. Simply, "if you can hold a pencil in place under your breast, you should never leave home without the support of a brassiere." Let's just say that growing up, that was one of the few tests I failed... or passed, depending on your point of view. That's not to say my young breasts were not perky—my girls looked straight ahead, not at all afraid to look you in the eye. They were also incredibly sensitive and the merest brush up against them would send me wincing. But it was the weight of the mammary glands that were my undoing. My teenage breasts could not only hold up a pencil, but they could also hold a full box of Ticonderoga #2's with ease. And worse, they continued to grow.

I won't go into all the awkward assumptions boys and men have when it comes to large breasted young women, but I will say they (the breasts, and the men) got me into a lot of situations and places I should not have been and garnered me a lot of attention I did not need and was ill equipped to handle.

Throughout my life, I don't think I have met more than a handful of women who love their breasts. They are too small, too large, too long, too uneven.

I once participated in a fundraiser that involved a group of women having casts made of our breasts that were then painted or otherwise decorated and then displayed in a local coffee shop. Afterwards, they were auctioned off to raise awareness and funding for breast cancer research.

I walked into a room full of women standing naked from the waist up, hands above their heads, much as we do when we go through airport security. Other women were applying strips of plaster to the torso and breasts to create the plaster casts. As I assumed the hands above heads position, feeling a little bit self-conscious and praying I was not the reason they ran out of plaster, the conversation centered around the topic of how very different each of our breasts were and our unhealthy relationship with them. "My boobs are so saggy," said one woman. "That's what happens when you have someone sucking on them every day for two years," responded another. "I know," cried a third. "I keep telling my husband to stop, but he won't!" We all laughed out loud.

Breasts are not merely ornamental. They support life. They are part of our sexuality. They can become part of our identity. But each of us, from the breast-feeding mom suffering from engorgement to the older lady with barely a fried egg sized bosom, we complained. When a woman who had undergone a double mastectomy disrobed, we all became quiet. "It makes for a flat canvas," she quipped, putting us all at ease.

Her plaster mold later transformed into a beautiful landscape in acrylics. Meanwhile, mine became a chip and dip set.

Decades later I look at these formerly firm globes that were practically their own life form in disbelief. "The girls" became part of my character, often garnering attention but not always the attention I sought, they were a bit like having a friend who is also a belligerent drunk. Fun but trouble. They enticed men, nourished children, and were intrinsically tied to my identity ("You know, the girl with brown eyes and huge boobs") and now I realize they have quit the game!

Gravity is winning with an inevitable pull toward Earth.

It is not a total shock. I assumed I would have issues with sagging breasts decades ago, while still breastfeeding my youngest. Full and firm as my mammary glands were at the time, I realized I was in trouble when one began to leak, and my thigh got wet. It's been pretty downhill since then.

Today my breasts no longer have that "look you in the eye" confidence but rather portray one who is lacking self-esteem— head down, bent low wallflowers, swaying to and fro. They are the needy friends who demand constant support and systemic structure. The brasseries in my drawer are so sturdy they stand on their own. And they take up a lot of space. I'm talking four to five clasps in the back, straps a half inch wide and enough underwire to fence a garden.

When I come home from anywhere, my first move is to remove the confining apparatus. Massaging the indentation at my shoulders, I watch as "the girls'" drop from chest height to stomach, inching their way closer to my bellybutton with each passing day.

It's a natural part of the aging process, I suppose. I could have opted for surgery of course, a lift or a reduction, but when it comes to this journey, I've opted for the natural progression.

I am humbled, though part of me feels a bit betrayed. Hour after hour and year after year, no matter how diligent the workout regimen is, there is no denying the course of an aging body. No amount of rowing is going to perk this bust back up to where it began.

There was a time when I thought of my breasts much as good friends. They helped me feed my children. They took me places! We had some good times. Now I see them as quitters. It takes just one look in the mirror to understand. There is no denying it and no defending it—these boobies are not even trying anymore!

Hollie Grimaldi-Flores

"C" is for Change

This chapter could easily have been titled "courage" as there is little question that it takes courage to fight the good fight that is the aging process. But, for women, especially, our bodies are everchanging and do require a bit of "girding the loins". I mean, the changes are never ending!

We kick off puberty with the monthly ability to bleed for a week without dying. For many of my generation, that first sign of our transition from girl to woman was also a bit scary because chances were pretty good that no one told us what was coming!

I think I missed gym class the day they showed "the film" that explained our changing bodies, but my older siblings had let me in on the secret. Many of my peers were not so fortunate.

One friend shared that she kept finding stains on her panties and threw several pairs out before finally going to her mother out of fear. Her mom laughed and then taught her how to use a tampon.

While I understood what was happening, when I found blood on my underwear that fateful sixth grade day and went to my mother, she helped me in a clinical fashion. At that time, we wore thick pads that were held in place with a garter belt like contraption. She strapped me in and said simply, "This is not something you talk about to boys." I was on my way out to the roller rink with several "couples" from school and thought, "How do I keep the fact that I am straddling a mattress a secret?" It was uncomfortable and awkward and in one sentence, my mother managed to make it feel dirty.

I never got over the shame that came with having my period. I simply did not talk about it to the male species. Even after marriage. Even after childbirth.

I asked several women what the experience of the everchanging body was like for them and now have a long laundry list of things "no one told us", from what to expect when we started menstruating to what happens when we give birth to what menopause might have in store for us.

No one mentioned that for many of us, hair would stop growing under our arms and legs, but instead take root on our chin or neck (which honestly may have been my chin just a year prior).

No one mentioned that just because your mom had an easy "change of life" you would not necessarily have the same experience.

No one mentioned that a regular period would become quite irregular at the onset of menopause or that some cycles would be so heavy, you would wish for one of those old mattress/maxi pads of yesteryear. There were days I didn't feel safe leaving the house!

No one mentioned that menopause would last decades, but that is for a later chapter (see M).

In between that first period and the last (also known as "the change"), many women manage to grow another human inside their bodies. Talk about courage. Of course, we heard about morning sickness and read all about "what to expect while we were expecting", but I may have missed the chapter that mentioned during the push phase of the birthing process, there might be excrement!

"Just wait," was the war cry of my elders. "It's incredibly painful."

Yes. Yes, it is. Only courageous women have done it and by that, I mean, if you have given birth, you are, indeed a woman of courage, be it reluctantly or willingly, giving birth should come with an award!

Yes, I know that in theory, the child is the reward, but I am talking about a spa day, or jewelry and not years of sleep deprivation or thankless sacrifice. Parenthood is the toughest job out there, and I am certain someone did try to warn me about it, but until you are in it, you just cannot fully grasp the magnitude of the change that has taken place.

Here is another area that changes and is never really discussed: coughing and laughing. The older I get, the more challenging these two circumstances. It took a while, but I now know that if I am about to do either, I need to be standing still with legs crossed.

The leaking! Ladies! Who is with me on this? From a tiny drip to a full-on gush, the bladder weakens with age. Someone should have told us!

The internal physical changes, while in a league of their own, barely compare to what happens on the outside.

Most of the older women I grew up around only offered

this bit of ominous wisdom: "Just you wait!"

I sure would have appreciated a few more details.

"D" is for Death

One thing I know for sure, is that if you live long enough, you will be doing some dancing with death. Death comes for all of us and is such a mystery.

A year of what I called "peripheral grief" just took place. All around me, people I dearly love were grieving the unexpected loss of spouses and friends. One to a heart attack and another, an expected-but-not-so-quick death to cancer. The latter, possibly a blessing for the pain that lovely woman was in but so hard for those she left behind.

Death comes for us all but without a real timeline, it seems. There's little predicting when one will die or how. Who lives and who dies comes without reason. Really good people gone too soon. Really bad people still walking the planet tormenting those in their path. Good or bad, there is no escaping it. Eventually, it takes us all.

The longer I am on this Earth, the more likely I will be here to mourn the passing of those I know and love. There is the "natural" passing of parents – many of us will experience this at some point. But then there is the unnatural passing of children first – something I never want to suffer firsthand!

There are myriad ways for our time in this realm to come to an end.

I personally vote for old age and natural causes but only if I know I am still in the room! There's an old joke about dying in my sleep like Grandpa did, not screaming in panic like the passengers in his car. Funny? Not funny? The notion of living to a ripe old age – long enough to see my children grow and to watch them raise families of their own is my ideal. But here is another side to that coin.

My mother-in-law is about to turn 96. She still lives on her own, in the childhood home of my husband. She has ailments here and there but remains surprisingly independent, with a strong Catholic faith. She says she is ready to meet her maker and to reap the promise of eternal life as she ardently believes and is here until God decides to take her. She grieves daily for those who have already died including her parents, her husband, her only sibling and too many relatives to count. Her pain continues with the loss of every close friend she ever had.

Losing family is hard, and losing friends is hard.

Both of my parents have passed on, as have two of my siblings. I have lost a close friend to a surgery gone wrong, and lost another, who was part of my adopted family of friends to the long goodbye also known as dementia.

The losses are painful. The lessons to be learned, often mysterious.

I have watched those I love dance with death in the form of cancer and wrote about it several times in a column I write for the local newspaper.

This is one of those essays…

"Like many of you, I love a person who is living with cancer. Living with cancer is the preferred phrase in our circle – fighting cancer, battling cancer, or receiving treatment for cancer are other ways of acknowledging the condition, but we don't say "dying of cancer" … at least, not today.

It's been six years since I received a call telling me to get to the hospital. My friend had been having trouble swallowing for a couple of months and then one day, he couldn't see. A trip to the ER and some tests followed. The diagnosis was not a good one: Stage 4 Cancer (meaning tumors and markers in multiple locations); a six-month prognosis. I sat on the end of his hospital bed with other friends also sitting vigil. He said he was not ready to die. My recollection was turning to him to say, "Well, you aren't dying today." And with that, I climbed down to the banks of that river known as denial and stayed put.

His recollection is different. He remembers coming home from the hospital and wallowing in self-pity and fear, barely able to get out of bed. He and his wife allowed themselves some time to grieve and then he says he woke up one day and said, "I might be dying, but I am not dying today." He made the decision to get back to living.

Either memory, his or mine, and likely a few others, have led us to the "not today" slogan we call on when things take a turn for the not so great. When treatments stop working or energy is lagging or the bright side is hard to find, we can focus on the present, take it one day at a time and be grateful for another day of living.

At this point we've known each other for over 20 years. Our children brought us together when they became fast friends in daycare. Long after the kids stopped wanting to hang out, we dragged them on vacations and playdates and other activities because by then we had become family. I am not good at losing people I love. I tend to hold on tight.

He has been the topic of a column or two in the past, always unnamed, but he would occasionally recognize a familiar tale about him (like the time he was first diagnosed, and I wrote about it) or a family member and asked me to refrain from sharing personal details without permission. I have honored his request, so I was a little surprised when he asked if we could meet because he had something for me to write about.

He's been beating the odds for a while now and thinks he's been living with the disease long enough to have some wisdom to impart on those of us who have no idea how receiving a terminal diagnosis might feel. I know I don't know anything about what hearing those words might do to me. I also know I sometimes don't know what to say to others who have it, so as a public service, from someone who does understand, here are a few key points he would like you to consider:

Don't compare your cancer. "I had a little melanoma, and my doctor removed it, just like that," or a hundred other cancer stories are not helpful. Your friend's cancer experience, your relative's cancer experience, your friend's relative's cancer experience, is not the same as another person's cancer experience.

Don't suggest treatments that worked for a friend or relative. Everyone wants to be an expert when it comes to what will work for my friend's cancer. Have you tried…? Or don't try… are a) none of your business and b) not helpful. Each person who receives a diagnosis needs to do their own soul searching and research. You may think you would never go through or try any number of options, but until you are staring cancer in the face, you really do not know.

Don't be disappointed when they outlive the prognosis. It sounds incredulous, but there have been instances of folk who seem put out. "I thought you were dying, man. You don't look sick." Should he be apologizing here?

Don't say, "everyone is going to die." I admit to being guilty of making this statement. My friend says there is a huge difference between knowing we are all going to die someday and knowing something in your body is actively killing you or receiving an end date from your oncologist.

Don't be afraid to talk about it or ask how things are going, but don't let it be the only topic.

And to that point, I'm sure there are more pieces of advice he could offer but we got distracted as we so often do when we are together and ended up talking about other important issues of the day, which leads me to things you can do when you have a loved one living with a terminal disease.

Do the things you enjoy doing together, now. Say yes to invitations. Buy them flowers. Say what you have been meaning to say. Take the trip. Book the hotel. Buy the tickets. Go on walks. Watch sunrises and sunsets. Drink the good wine. Take the drive. Sit in stillness. Be present. Live like you are dying!

I haven't had a chance to tell him yet, but I decided to look up the "hashtag not today" on the web and found the phrase was popularized before either of us had our epiphany around it. It turns up in the much-acclaimed series "Game of Thrones," and throughout the series where the saying gained attention, beginning in Season 1, in 2011 when master swordfighter Syrio Forel said to Arya Stark during her training. "There is only one God, and His name is Death. And there is only one thing we say to Death: 'not today'.

Those folks were onto something………"

More than six years after that six months to live diagnosis but just ten weeks after this published, my friend was dead. His last words to me were "See you on the other side". I sure hope so!

I asked him to let me know if he could that he was okay, and he said he would find me at the beach. I have seen dolphins swimming offshore on two separate occasions at a beach we would frequent with our families though I had never seen them there before his passing. I love that. Maybe it's merely a strange coincidence or the result of rising ocean temperatures, but I choose to believe his spirit lives on. It gives me comfort. I love believing in the possibility that our loved ones are able to let us know they are still around us.

What these experiences have taught me is that it is important to live a good life. And the beauty of it is that the definition of "good life" is yours to define! Do you want to spend your days in the mountains or in the desert or at the beach? Are you someone who loves the bustle of city life or prefers a remote homestead or somewhere in between? If travel is your thing, travel. Run for political office. Teach. Spend every night out with friends or every night curled up on the sofa. It's all up to you. Say yes to what feels good to you and live life as if there is no tomorrow.

We can go kicking and screaming or we can dance our way there, either way, it may not be today, but death comes for us all. I hope you dance.

"E" is for Exercise

"Use it or lose it" has never been truer than with the aging mind and body. I am in awe of the sheer number of senior citizens I see exercising – on bikes, hiking on trails, attending classes at various gyms around town, on the increasingly popular Pickleball Courts. My body is not/has not been well trained. Though I know it is an important part of a daily routine if I truly desire quality in the last chapter of this life. I really have tried.

I was never much of an athlete unless you count "try athlete" meaning I would try, just about anything. I tried softball but had no hand-eye coordination whatsoever. "That's a swing and a miss, Miss."

The same was true for volleyball, tennis, even billiards. Bowling was an exception because there were arrows to help line up the ball. My skill vastly improved when I finally got eyeglasses. I realized those dots at the end of the lane showing which pins were left standing were visible and clear for all who played the game, and not just a blurry set of lights decorating the end of the alley.

Basketball was definitely not my thing, though I did okay with H.O.R.S.E. in the back driveway of a neighbor's house.

Skiing was too expensive. Gymnastics and dance required grace and coordination I did not possess. I tried them all thanks to gym classes throughout my formative years.

Swimming was a challenge, and though I am awkward, even in water, it was one form of exercise I found to be doable. I had lung capacity! An aquatics requirement in college was fulfilled with a scuba diving class, but buoyancy (back to "B" for breasts) issues required a weight belt in the pool. Diving into cold water (Syracuse, NY in January) kept me from my open water certification. At the time, Onondaga Lake was also known as the most polluted lake in America. Really, there was nothing in that body of water I needed to see. By skipping out on that polar plunge, I feel like I made a healthier choice!

Organized sports never became a thing for me.

Pickleball is all the rage these days with the older set, and I understand it is keeping orthopedic surgeons incredibly busy. The competitive senior must remember that the path from thinking it to moving it is no longer a direct line. By the time the brain registers the need to turn the knee, the knee has lost. Still, I'd give it a whirl.

I am a joiner! In truth, I was usually game to try any of it and would stumble through my lack of coordination for a time, but I was rarely asked back, never first to be picked for a team, and nothing ever really "took" except walking, as I mentioned in the letter "A".

Walking with a friend where the talking is therapy and eight to ten thousand steps the side benefit.

Walking does nothing for my upper body strength or my stomach, so the skin sags and it's difficult to do a sit up, but my legs are strong, calves large and firm, and my heart surely appreciates the effort.

And then there is running. My husband is a runner. He was an ultra-marathon runner and has participated in treks of 26.2 miles or more 95 times. His goal is 100 but bad knees and an aching back may leave him short. He ran his first marathon in San Francisco at the age of 27. He has run ultra-marathons (50K or 31-plus miles) and finished the Western States Endurance Run (100 miles.) He runs six days a week without fail. It does not matter where we are or what the weather is like or how he is feeling. He runs. His biggest current complaint is that while he ran his first marathon in just a bit over three hours, he will have to fight to finish his next one in under six. His body refuses to keep up with a mind that is firmly running away from the aging process.

I am not a runner. I have attempted running, and while I have entered a few 5Ks (3.1 miles), I always end up walking for at least part of it.

I took an eight-week course called, "Train to Run," thinking if I could just get my breathing and form under control, it would be more enjoyable. It was not. I worked on my posture, my breathing, and where I placed my feet while learning to pump my arms for the greatest benefit. It did not get easier. It took a solid year of training before I could run one mile without stopping.

I yearned for the "runner's high," but was recently informed that does not come until after at least three miles of consistent running, and since I only run three miles, well, you get the picture. I have been told it would be easier for me to run if I lost weight, and it would be easier for me to lose weight if I just ran. A paradox for sure.

My reality is that I do not have a runner's body. I am not

built to run. I think I am built to farm—ancestrally speaking.

And while I do not profess to be any kind of poet, I did pen this little ditty as a gift to the runner in my life:

I want to run—run away with you.
But from the porch to the driveway is the best I can do.
My calves are cramping. My knees are weak.
My thighs are chafing and my hips, well, creak.
I have bought the right shoes. And undergarments, like armor.
Seems my chest and my chin are not fond of each other.
The bouncing. The bruising. The burn in my lung.
There's pain in my back, that will not be undone.
I want to run, you know that I do, but first.
I choose a bath, some ice, and an aspirin—or two.

Don't let my angst dissuade you. If you are so inclined and find the satisfaction that comes with it, keep putting one foot in front of the other. I can't say I will ever understand this love of running, but I can say it is difficult not to be in awe of the discipline and fortitude it takes for those who do.

Exercise in whatever form you can manage is better than no exercise at all. As we age, it can only help so I will keep looking for the something, that works for me. But right now, I am going to exercise my right to sit here and do nothing.

"F" is for Forgetful

The old adage "a mind is a terrible thing to waste" (or lose) is not completely lost on me. All that partying in my youth may have resulted in a shortage of viable cells in these later decades.

Things just don't come to me as easily and "what the F?" is a daily mantra. Maybe that is the "f" – this getting older is really not for sissies. It requires focus and fortitude. Lots of "f's" to consider.

My children's greatest fear when it comes to me getting older is that I will develop Alzheimer's or some other form of dementia. We hear the term dementia and think the worst, but what does it really mean?

According to an online article published by AARP, "In the simplest terms, dementia is a decline in mental function—thinking, remembering, and reasoning—that is usually irreversible," notes neurologist Ron Petersen, M.D., director of the Mayo Clinic Alzheimer's Disease Research Center and the Mayo Clinic Study of Aging in Rochester, Minnesota. "The catchall phrase encompasses several disorders that cause chronic memory loss, personality changes or impaired reasoning, Alzheimer's disease being just one of them. What it's not? Typical mild forgetfulness that sometimes accompanies aging—say, having trouble remembering the name of an acquaintance who comes up to you on the street. In fact, the earliest stage of dementia, known as mild cognitive impairment (MCI), is considered "forgetfulness beyond what is expected from aging."

So, in a nutshell, as we age, we become forgetful. It's natural. It doesn't mean we'll be living like Gena Rowland in "The Notebook" (if you have never seen it, do). It can be a natural part of our aging process and may never get any worse than it is right now.

A few years ago, my husband and I set off for a week at a beach on the opposite side of the country, leaving the care of the house and cat to one of our offspring. Grateful to have them old enough to do so, and old enough to do so without some outrageous party taking place while we are away—as was the case a decade prior when we went on a cruise to celebrate my 50th birthday. We were heading to points south when I saw a social media post of a young girl balancing on a rafter that looked suspiciously like the one that runs across the living room in our log home. Years later we learned that party would go down in our children's extended circle as an unforgettable, epic memory, but I digress.

This time, we rested easy, knowing both abode and pet were in good hands. They even picked us up from the airport, saving us dollars on parking and time finding our way to the vehicle. The trip itself was forgettable. I picked a white sandy beach town known more for spring break than for what I really had in mind, which was tiki bars with buskers playing "Brown Eyed Girl" or "A Pirate Looks at Forty." We made the best of it and had a relatively low-key time eating and drinking our way through each day. It is another place I never need to visit again, but still, a nice getaway.

But don't let me now forget where I was headed with this: After picking us up at arrivals and driving the 60 plus miles back home making small talk and recapping our time away, we pulled into the driveway, when our driver said, nonchalantly as you please, "By the way, I had read one of the ways to stave off memory loss is to change things up, so I rearranged all the contents of all the cupboards and drawers in the kitchen. Welcome home!"

"You what?" was our initial response. We spent the next several weeks with mixed reactions. For one, several of the choices made much better sense. The pans should have always been there, what were we thinking? Oh, the glasses fit so much better here, etc.

For others it was like being on a search and find mission or required a text to the remodeler, "Where are the measuring cups?"

Then there was the frequent exclamation, "Damn it!" when habit would send us opening the wrong drawer for the hundredth time looking for a fork, even though we knew and liked where the cutlery was now housed.

Habits are hard to form and hard to break. I'm not sure the tactic did anything to keep my mind intact, but it did help with organization and purging. Storage containers with long missing lids were gone!

People asked if I was upset, but how could I be, realizing what an arduous chore it turned out to be, taking hours to accomplish, and knowing it came from a place of love.

It's that place of love that will stay with me. It's the love I will never forget.

I have no way of knowing what the future has in store for me when it comes to my brain. I think the best approach is to keep using it and to continue making memories that will last a lifetime.

"G" is for Gratitude

This is a lesson that has come with getting older. Gratitude makes all things possible. I have kept a journal most of my life, and I noticed the biggest shift in my outlook came when I decided to start each entry with gratitude, first and foremost.

Initially, I struggled with repeating the same basic things over and over. I'm grateful for a roof over my head, grateful for reliable transportation, grateful for my good health and the good health of my loved ones. What else was there? But over time, two things happened. First, I realized I should be incredibly grateful for what I considered to be "the basics". How lucky was I to have a roof over my head, reliable transportation, and good health? Not everyone could say the same thing on any given day.

Secondly, my viewpoint began to expand, and I was able to acknowledge and express gratitude for even more basic gifts that would often get overlooked—the smell of rain, the sound of birds, the softness of the fur on my cat, the peacefulness of a quiet house. My list grew, expanding to pages some days, and back to a few sentences on other mornings.

Over time, my viewpoint shifted. My outlook improved.

More good things came my way.

I know I didn't always take the time to appreciate the good in my life. There were long stretches when it was much easier to focus on all that was going wrong. It may be in our nature, but I found the more I focused on the negative, the more negative there was to be found!

While clearing through some old books, I found a letter I had written to myself when I was about 16 years old. According to my note, I was having trouble sleeping, and as was my habit, decided to write to myself to sleep. I think at that time in my life, writing was a tool I used to soothe and quiet my restless mind.

Finding the letter was especially meaningful for a few reasons. First, I do not recall writing it or having seen it since that night. I have no idea how it ended up between the pages of a book I managed to hold onto for all these years. Second, all my journals written prior to my mid-twenties were stolen during a breakup. My former boyfriend took them when I was moving out. I have no idea what became of them, but since I have yet to recognize my tales of angst in the published world, I can only surmise they were tossed into the garbage. It was a horrendous violation and simply reinforced my decision to end the relationship. Thus, this single sheet of paper written by the teenage version of me truly is a gift I may never have discovered if not for COVID cleaning. Finally, something about the 2020 shutdown for which I can be grateful!

In the first paragraph of the letter, I explained my inability to sleep and then went on to list several of my shortcomings including, sadly, my need to lose weight. Oh, those teen years! Luckily, my journaling that night took a turn toward gratitude. I listed my circle of friends as blessings and reminded myself of the many positives in my life. There was mention of the recent death of a fellow student (who I cannot recall), which gave me pause, and the understanding that life was fleeting. Even then, I understood the uncertainty of the human condition and pledged to live a full life! I shared the realization that even though some things were less than stellar at home, in my core I was happy, loved and supported by my friends—and the family I created for myself.

After tucking the letter away, I thought about what I would say to that girl today. There is no way that that girl could have imagined the experiences that would unfold over the many decades that have passed since, and life—as it stands today—is beyond comprehension.

My grandparents survived the Spanish Flu. My parents survived the Great Depression. My siblings lived through the Civil Rights Movement. Who would have ever predicted living through a pandemic, financial crisis and human rights uprising concurrently?

During the pandemic I was taxed with the struggle to adjust to the "new normal". Each day, I would wake up with any number of approaches to the day. I ran the emotional gamut. One day feeling optimistic. Another day, I would awaken with a feeling of utter hopelessness. There were days I felt incredibly resilient followed by moments of utter despair. Ultimately, I found my way to the sunny side and put one foot in front of the other, finding the good side of whatever situation each day presented, which was not always easy, but was absolutely essential. And as I do with all things, I assured myself and those around me that "this too shall pass."

Against my own common sense and advice of those wiser than me, I watched, read, listened, and spent way too much time on social media, following the news of the day.

Headlines baited me, and if I went down a rabbit hole, it was easy to get lost in there for hours.

But it was deep in the folds that I discovered a lovely surprise. Though the headlines walked us down a doomsday path of corruption and hopelessness, the smaller print was full of the opposite—stories of people helping people.

Tales of honor and survival. That is where I chose to focus.

There was so much uncertainty, and the entire world was struggling. Naively, I believed this virus would come and go and life would return to normal in a matter of weeks.

The task was to find a way to not only survive, but to also enjoy life as we were living it. What we thought we could endure paled beside the reality of several years of uncertainty. But survive, we did.

It got me thinking about what I would say to that 16-year-old girl who had trouble sleeping on a late spring night in upstate New York:

Dear teenager me,

You have a bright future along a bumpy road ahead of you. Be kind to yourself.
Your friends and family (including the family you create for yourself) are your most valuable assets.
Material goods are replaceable. People—not so much.
Give more than you take.
Get outside often.
Be gentle with yourself and your spirit.
Learn from those who have lived longer and have more experience.
Don't let fear of failure stop you from going after your

dreams.
Learn from your mistakes. Don't waste energy berating yourself for making them.
Trust your instincts.
Know you are enough, just the way you are.
Dark days will come but will always, always, give way to brighter seasons.
Spend time at the beach.
Hike into the hills.
Say "yes" as often as possible.
And one last thing: Buckle up, sister, 2020 is going to be a wild ride which you will survive.

With Love,
Still here and over sixty me

It's not bad advice, but I forgot one thing:
Above all else, be grateful.

"H" is for Hot

That would be hot, as in flash! Just a minute ago, I was seamlessly comfortable. It was one of those early summer mornings when the temperature was just about perfect, but then I felt that now familiar rise of heat, beginning with my upper lip and moving through my body like a miniature furnace. The infamous hot flash took hold for a moment and passed almost as quickly, for now, but this has been going on for years and years, closing in on a decade at this point. I had heard through social lore that women suffered hot flashes while going through menopause, but I do not recall hearing hot flashes made encore appearances for decades after "the change" reached completion!

Don't get me wrong, I firmly believe there is a time and a place for a good old fashioned hot flash—take winter, for example. I do not like to be cold, so when I first experienced my own internal flames, I embraced it. Let 'em see me sweat! I didn't mind, not that there was much I could do about it anyway.

The internal workings of the female anatomy are mind boggling.

We bring new life catapulting into the world from a tiny opening between our legs that can expand to the size of a watermelon in a matter of hours and then return (mostly) to the original size.

Meanwhile our bodies transform throughout our life span.

Medically, research on women's health is greatly underfunded and, in its infancy, compared to what has been explored for men.

There is still so much we do not know.

When I was young, my mother was uncomfortable talking about the changes that were happening to our bodies. As I was entering puberty, she was experiencing hormonal changes associated with a hysterectomy. I'd love to tell you why my mother opted to have her uterus removed in her early 40's but I do not know the answer. The reason I do not know the reason is because when I asked my mom about it, her answer was "Because my doctor told me I needed to have one."

Previous generations were not taught to question the authority of the medical community. "Take the little yellow pill when you are tired, take the little blue pill when you can't sleep. Get the hysterectomy because I said so."

Granted we have come a long way (I hope) from my mother's generation. Each year more money is allocated to fund research on women's health issues. My daughter is more confident and comfortable with her body. She is willing to discuss her health with me and professionals and will do her own research to make up her own mind.

She is not likely to have any procedure based on a "because they said so" and I am so proud of her for bucking the status quo—for questioning that which does not sit well with her and for exploring the best options that feel right for her.

Though none of that is going to change the fact that she, too, will one day go through a change of her own, it is encouraging to know she will be more informed about what to expect when she does.

One of my first experiences of the (until then, mythical) hot flash came to me in a staff meeting. My employer held a weekly "standing meeting" to keep them short and sweet. We literally stood in a circle around the conference table and gave a quick round of each department head's day. I was giving my report when the heat began to rise from the depths of my being. I could feel the flush and the sweat. I thought I'd had a bad donut—those cream filled ones can be tricky—but almost as quickly as the onset, my body temperature dropped back down to normal. No one asked if I was okay, so, I'm guessing my imagination painted a more dramatic picture than my reality. "Oh," I thought to myself.

"So, this is what all the hoopla is about! That wasn't so bad." Ha!

Soon, the flashes were coming on with a bit of regularity but without a discernable pattern, though I quickly began counting on them to get me through cold nights. They would come on in the wee hours, waking me from a fitful sleep. I'd spend most hours throwing blankets onto my husband, only to retrieve them a few minutes later, chilled to the bone. He would make comments about how the heat coming off my frame would cause him to break into a sweat. He'd back away from spooning and flip to the outer edge of his side of the bed, leaving me drenched in sweat, changing, or simply removing my night garments, wiping sweat from my brow and cleavage and soon enough I'd be shivering into the chilly, winter night.

Every woman should receive a personal fan when she turns 50, along with a wide berth, for that matter!

The ever-changing physiology of the female human is fascinating. Blame it on the hormonal fluctuations, but we have every right to be a tad bit moody. Puberty and the next forty odd years are a non-ending cycle (thus the term cycle) and then, when the cycles run dry and reproduction is no longer viable, we get hormonal "Jenga"— one wrong move and the entire tower could all come crashing down! It feels like we are on the brink of disaster. I mean, what is next? Women experience changes in hair growth, thickness, body fat that can only be resolved surgically, weight gain, sleeplessness, mood swings and let us not forget, hot flashes!

Aging is not for the faint of the heart may be one of our culture's biggest understatements.

And I have a lot more to say about that, but hang on while I turn my personal fan to high and wait for the sweat on my upper lip to dissipate.

"I" is for Intimacy

I did not see this one coming. As a young woman, it is fair to say that I had a healthy appetite for sex—or the connection that came with sex. Suffice it to say, in the late 1970's to mid-1980's, I took advantage and was taken advantage of, without hesitation or boundaries. From spin the bottle and practice kissing, to the back seat fumbling of teens in lust, to the promiscuous experimentation, instant gratification, and search for what I thought equated to love, to the sometimes frantic and prolific desire, to finally experiencing the joy and pain of real, true intimacy and the vulnerability that it requires, I spent a lot of time getting physical.

Intimacy is allowing the truest parts of yourself to be exposed and shared with your partner. It is letting down all the walls and, in my opinion, the most important ingredient to a successful partnership.

When my husband and I were dating, we could not keep our hands off each other and stole moments anywhere and everywhere we could manage. Morning, noon and night—lunchtime trysts, evening sneak aways, making out in the car, lingering on the porch before finally saying goodnight. Those were the days.

We spent the first ten years of our marriage balancing our desire with navigating the lack of privacy that comes with having children constantly coming and going.

We put a lock on our bedroom door but were not always great about making sure the door latched tightly. I remember one evening we were in the throes of passion, finding ourselves contorted in shape and directions I had not known possible when the door suddenly flew open and we saw our 10-year-old daughter standing in the doorway, momentarily frozen in her tracks before she slowly began backing away.

I quickly grabbed a robe, covered myself and went to her room.

With her back to me she simply put up her hand in a "don't take another step toward me" fashion. "I told you, you have to knock," I said gently. "I did," she answered, still not turning my way. "I thought you said come in." With that, I backed away myself, thinking it was entirely possible she heard something that sounded very close to that. I held back my laughter and tried to comfort her.

Now in her late 20's, she still talks about the trauma of realizing her parents actually had sex!

"That is something I will never unsee," she recounts!

Fast forward a couple of decades and the daily physical connection has slowed down from frantic to a more sedate "every now and then" pace. We have both rejected and been rejected by each other.

We've navigated grown children. With an empty nest, we now have nothing but opportunity to copulate which cruelly met up with my post-menopausal body and general lack of interest in revving that engine. The desire hormones are depleted, and with it, intimacy has shifted from the purely physical nature to one of familiarity.

Our intimacy now comes in the form of our shared history and is communicated with a knowing look from across a room filled with friends, or a gentle touch as we make dinner together.

Holding hands while watching television and kissing goodnight may be as physical as we get for too long a stretch. We assure each other that all is well, but it's easy to fall toward the too tired or too lazy or simply not being interested enough to make the effort.

We are entwined in a way that allows intimacy without touch, but now labor to find our way back to desire and passion, if for no other reason than to make sure all the parts still work!

In my husband's defense, I will confess this is at least 85% me exhibiting a lack of interest. He is still very interested in a robust physical display of affection, to a fault! Life is so unfair in the distribution of drive.

I am told hormones are to blame and I am certain they play a factor. In all honesty, there is also the reality of what comes with sharing life with someone for multiple decades. Face it, we kind of know what is coming next. Not as mundane as step one followed by steps two and three, but it is fair to say we have shown our best moves and played our best hand more than a time or two.

Keeping things spicey comes back to effort and energy, and I know that it is what we allow it to be. We are familiar with each other in a way no other person on the planet is familiar with either of us—not our parents or siblings or closest friends. We allowed each other to see the underbelly. We know what makes each other tick. We know where the buttons are and push them at will. We know how to give and how to take. And we are still happy to be a couple.

Intimacy comes in a variety of forms—it's not all about exchanging fluids. True intimacy comes in the form of communication. There is comfort in knowing and being known so deeply, and that is an intimacy I would not trade.

"J" is for Joy

As I age, that which brings me joy has made a shift. I am joyful after eight hours of uninterrupted sleep. Joyful when my back does not ache, when heat does not flash, when digestion is smooth and regular, when knees and ankles bend as they were designed. It doesn't take much.

Joy comes in the form of a grandson who is busy exploring the world from a relatively new and unsteady walking perspective.

Joy is spending an afternoon with my adult children over a meal, at a local river, or on the back deck listening to stories about their lives.

Joy comes while planning a trip to the coast, after going too long without experiencing the calmness that emanates from watching waves crashing endlessly against the rocks at my favorite beach.

Joy comes in the peace of knowing there is food in the pantry, money in the bank, gas in my car and propane in the tank.

Finding joy in the small things and letting the euphoria wash over me without qualification is a skill honed with age.

It is simple and attainable. Here is my list of just a few things that bring me joy:

- Babies
- Beaches
- Hummingbirds
- Time with my kids
- Travel
- Girlfriends
- Spontaneous getaways with my spouse
- Spontaneous getaways without my spouse
- Live Music
- Watching karaoke
- Cooking
- Eating
- Drinking with friends
- Parties
- Playing word games and word puzzles.
- Boating
- Planning—parties, trips, surprises, etc.

For many, many years I was a happiness seeking junkie. I worked at being the bright light walking into a room. I took as much pleasure in being funny as I did in laughing at others' humor and said yes to any experience that sounded the least bit pleasant. And I spent decades suffering from mild to clinical depression.

I went to therapy and learned that happiness lives on the outside. My counselor, at the time, suggested simply being content was a worthy goal. I wanted more.

Joy, I believe, is not an outward expression, but rather comes from within. It runs deep and it is a practice. Taking the time to do things that bring peace and feel good on the inside is long lasting and, I truly believe, a vital component to a life worth living.

What brings you joy? Name it. Claim it. Seek it. Prioritize it. The effect is long lasting, and it really is good for you. There is joy in knowing that.

Hollie Grimaldi-Flores

"K" is for Kids

As I get older, so do my children. The job of raising them is over but the job of parenting never really ends. I think, looking at them now, that I did a pretty good job. At this age, with all this hard-earned wisdom, I would likely do more than a few things differently, but there is the paradox: raising children at this age would be incredibly difficult – ask any of the increasing number of grandparents who are doing just that– but when we are young, we simply don't yet have the life experience to have many of the answers to the never ending questions required to do the job. We do the best we can with what we know and, hopefully, in the words of Maya Angelou, "When we know better, we do better.".

A case in point: I was having lunch with a girlfriend when an off-hand remark between the friend and one of my (now) adult children have me wondering if I was half the parent, I thought I was. The topic was school and paperwork and more specifically, parental signatures. My offspring confessed to spending quite a bit of time working on replicating my signature. The forgery, I was told, was to avoid getting into trouble. It was a matter of convenience.

They said my husband was never interested in signing documents and that I was never home to sign them, so rather than get in trouble for not turning something in, their signature became my signature.

"There was always a board meeting," they said, without blame or malice. It was stated innocently, as a point of fact. "Hmmm," I thought. "That's an interesting perspective." Later, I called my daughter and relayed the conversation. She concurred.

"But board meetings were only once a month," I said, quick to defend myself.

"Maybe there was more than one board," she replied. "There was always an event or something, Mom. You were busy."

I couldn't see it at the time. I never thought my volunteering or work would come with a price my kids had to pay. I prided myself on being all things to all people. Looking back, I see that yes, I was busy. I did sit on more than one board. I had a job that demanded time "after hours." I worked hard to be present in the community and attended more than my share of meetings and events.

My kids were right. There were a lot of "somethings" for more than a decade—a decade that included most of their school years.

While I felt conflicted, that conflict, I am certain, is the reason we are all here to talk about it now. Otherwise, I may not have survived those years. I may have gone crazy if my life consisted of nothing more than time at work and time at home.

The social creature in me needed so much more. During my early days of single parenting (which lasted for five years), I needed the support that came with being involved in my community. I joined a women's service organization, not with charity in mind, but out of a desperate need to make friends. My soon-to-be-ex-husband and I had moved to a new area just a year before the marriage came to an end. The need to connect with others, for me, was about survival, from finding babysitters to finding a supportive shoulder, I needed community! A lack of funds but an interest in participating in local events was resolved by volunteering at those events.

I thrived in the chaos of overcommitting. I took pride in how far I could stretch myself. A workday that often went 10 to 12 hours, followed by staffing a booth at a community event, or attending a council or board meeting or supporting another organization at a mixer or fundraiser was a source of validation.

I would run to the grocery store and somehow get dinner on the table before looking at schoolwork or whatever obligations home might have for me. Never to be accused of disregarding the children, I signed up to work in the classroom and chaperoned field trips.

Parenting is tough.

If I were to analyze it now (and you know that I am), I would say some part of that was my fear of losing who I was as a person in the world of being a mother. I saw it all around me—women who were so involved in the lives of their children that they had lost sight of who they were before someone called them Mom. In the back of my mind, I never forgot the fact that my children would grow up and move away. I needed to make sure there was something left of me to hold on to when they were gone.

In all fairness, no one is saying they were neglected. I remarried and my husband took on the role of school drop off king, so riding the bus was the exception rather than the norm. I packed lunches for years. He and I took turns cooking meals and made a point of having sit-down dinners with all the children several times a week—no easy task amid various sports and other after school activities.

I attended the plays, dozens of field trips and countless sporting events. I ran a free taxi service.

We hosted birthday sleepovers and playdates. I have been "team mom." My husband has been a youth sports coach for decades.

Do I sound defensive? I consider it a bit of soul searching. Did I find a balance between work and home? There are some who say, "You can have it all, but not all at once."

Having kids is a game changer that can never be fully explained. It is one of those circumstances that must be experienced to be fully understood. Not all of us are cut out for the job. I am happy to see my own kids deciding for themselves whether bringing life into this world is something they want to pursue. For my bio kids, we are tied with one "Hell, No!" and the other, "It can't happen soon enough." Both of those decisions are one hundred percent fine with me.

While my children were growing up, I put a lot of my desires on hold. I knew the time would come when I would be free to pursue more of my interests. That time is now. The kids are all adults and are, for the most part, doing just fine.

I like to think I am a living example of the importance of maintaining a life beyond the unending needs of my offspring. I hope I taught them the importance of pursuing a career they would love. I think they saw the value and impact volunteering can have, and that a job well done is the only one worth doing.

At the end of the day, I was there to tuck them in more often than I was not. I was there to listen and to lend support. They knew they were loved, and they always knew they were first in line when push came to shove.

They have grown into fine humans who, along with me, are getting a little older and a little wiser along the way. As it turns out, signing forms may not have been my strong suit, but they are no worse for it. They became problem solvers—and ones with very nice handwriting at that.

"L" is for Laughter

Is there anything better than good belly laughs? I am talking about full on tears to the eyes, legs crossed so you don't lose control, nonstop laughing. It's the best, and it's good for you. I was on an airplane the other day and heard the delightful squeal of a toddler laughing out loud over a tickle or an eye covered "boo" from the parent. The sound alone put a smile on my face!

Multiple studies have shown the average child laughs 300 times a day, while adults laugh only four to twenty times a day. That is quite a difference. Nothing funny about it. It's hard to deny the truth. Life is hard and it can certainly wear down the best of us.

But still, I love to laugh and seek funny situations. I am a sucker for a good stand-up comic and will almost always choose live comedy over other live entertainment options. As a matter of fact, I love to laugh so much, I grew my own comedian. The first born is working hard to make a career out of being funny. Talented and insightful, but still working as a server – talent and financial success do not always collide. While that is not necessarily funny, it is true!

A good sense of humor helps us recognize funny situations in everyday experiences from bad performances to bad karaoke, to humorous stage plays and readings— plenty of possibilities to express joy, happiness, or amusement. I highly recommend a daily guffaw.

Why does watching someone fall make most of us chuckle? A younger version of me found other's clumsiness hysterical, but now that I am of a certain age, I have come to know there is nothing funny about a fall.

Still, there are successful television programs focused on the humorous side of people tripping, falling, and generally wiping out. Failed attempts at stunts not only turn out to be hilarious, but also lucrative. "Who will win the $100,000, the guy who tripped into the baby pool or the lady who fell off her horse?"

I love a spontaneous response that can make my ribs ache and my eyes water. Yes, I love to laugh.

A good, hard laugh stays with me. The shared experience of a laugh is a deep connection. I remember getting kicked out of tenth grade English when a friend and I started giggling over something our teacher said and try as we might, we could not get our act together. Believe me, it has been decades, and I have lived several lives since walking the halls of my alma mater, but the memories of sidesplitting laughter stay with me far above the difficulties.

I still laugh when I think about the time my sister dove into the back of my car when a train whistle sent her into a panic, as if the locomotive was going to jump the track and run her down. The speed at which she was able to fling her body horizontally across the back seat was likened to that of a speeding locomotive. It doesn't translate well here, but you will have to take my word for the side-splitting belly laughs that followed.

A few years ago, a friend and I attended an independent film festival, watching foreign shorts. One of the submissions was an artsy black and white, without any dialogue, just music and the actions of a horse, a mule and a barking dog. I whispered something along the lines, "Hurry! Timmy is stuck in the well," to my companion who burst out a laugh, which sent me into a fit of giggles. Each time I heard her trying to control her emotions, I lost mine, again. The other adults in our vicinity were not amused. We would have left had we not been so close to the front of the theatre. Again, years later, and it still brings a smile to my face.

One of my favorite memories of spending time with my mother as an adult was when she and I attended a play together. It was a Sondheim musical and something about it amused my mother to the point of tears. Again, it was her contagious laughter that sent me into fits. She squeezed my hand tightly as she tried to bring her own emotions back into check, but we ended up leaving at intermission. I don't remember anything else about that evening, but I will always remember the sound of my mother laughing without control.

One of the last times I gathered with friends I have known most of my life, one off-hand comment from one of them at just the right time had me snorting the drink I was swallowing out through my nose. My friend and I fed off each other and were soon crossing our legs to control our increasingly weak bladders. I won't say here whether we were successful or not. Over the years that particular group of friends has been responsible for more than one side-splitting moment.

I spent a decade working as a broadcaster on a local, commercial radio station. In addition to bringing listeners the latest traffic, weather and local news, my morning partner and I would exchange and share many amusing anecdotes. His favorite thing to do was to time a punchline while I was taking a sip of coffee. Nothing amused him more than watching me spit out a beverage. It's been years since we worked together, but we can still each pull out a line that sends us both into a chuckle. There were more than a few.

Those examples are just a few and hopefully jarred a memory or two from you. The fact that I can pull up a half dozen moments of pure joy even decades after the fact speaks to the power of the events.

It is said that laughter is the best medicine, and it does come with many health benefits at any age.

Laughter is a great tool for relieving stress. A good intake of oxygen will stimulate your heart and lungs and send endorphins to the brain. It can increase your heart rate and then give a feeling of relaxation when the heartbeat slows back down. Over the long term, laughing can improve your overall mood, relieve pain, and even improve your immune system by generating more positive thoughts.

Of course, with my aging body comes the issue of bladder control. Who knew? There is a muscle in there and that muscle needs to be worked. The love of a good laugh and dry panties do not always go hand in hand! Still, I choose laughter.

Laughter may be the best medicine, but it must also be a virus, because it is contagious!

The next time you find yourself feeling a little blue, try watching a good comedy, or if you have one around, try playing peek-a-boo with a toddler.

"M" is for Many (including Menopause)

What word first comes to mind when you hear the "m" word? My first thought is money, but there are so many other "m" words affecting my day-to-day existence. Words such as marriage, music, men, muscle, memory, and muscle memory! All of those are great words to explore in detail but the "m" word I want to discuss today is a big one for the over-fifty female set. Yes, we are going to discuss menopause. Realizing this topic has been touched upon in previous chapters, I can sense the urge to skip the page, but bear with me.

I have a girlfriend I can hear yelling from downtown. "Don't ever talk about menopause," she said. "No one wants to hear about it." But I don't believe that is true. What is true, is that it is a word avoided too often, and I know I am not the only woman (or the men who love them) living with the reality of this process taking place in my aging body. It feels like another "m" word: mutiny!

Is there any word more accurately descriptive of what is happening daily than "mutiny" (n. an open rebellion)? This body of mine is no longer responsive or compliant in ways for which I was simply unprepared.

Certainly, we have all heard about hot flashes (see letter "H") which are most often laughed off in mixed company, but the reality of having a body that randomly bursts into flames is not something to be shrugged off. I didn't mind them so much in cold weather, but the novelty wore off when summer heat was already repressive. And when are they going to end?

The upside is that I am keeping my upper arms toned with the constant repetition of throwing blankets off my body and then pulling them back a few minutes later, over, and over, throughout the night. I would say slumber, but that would mean I am actually able to sleep.

Dealing with hot flashes is just the preview for the main event which comes in the form of insomnia. Sleep deprivation was first introduced to me after my first child was born. The big difference there is that I was sleeping soundly until the sound of a crying, hungry, and often, wet baby brought me from my rest. As my childbearing years ended, sleep became elusive, intermittent, and more like a stranger than a friend. And a bit ironic is the realization that now I do sleep like a baby—awake every two to three hours, famished and often soaking wet!

Another not so groovy part of this passage is the timeline. When does it end? About 20 years ago, during an annual exam, my doctor explained menopause is actually a four-part series that can last longer than Law & Order Special Victims Unit (now in its 23rd season).

First there is peri- which is when the body is thinking about the changes that will take place. And then there is pre- when things begin to get irregular, moods change, and bone density decreases, while cholesterol levels may skyrocket. All the while the hot flashes, night sweats, insomnia, muscle aches, and joint pain begin making intermittent appearances.

Eventually, actual menopause occurs which means we

are no longer able to bear children, and thus no longer, apparently, in need of estrogen, which comes with a new set of downers, such as dry skin, depression and fatigue.

We then spend the rest of our days in the post- state where the aforementioned are joined by their friends, hair loss, brittle bones, weight gain, difficulty concentrating and memory lapse. What is not to love?

Is it any wonder we are not as amorous as we once were? It's not that we have lost interest in our mates, per say. It's more like we have just lost interest! Frankly, with all the changes going on, it's a bit of a miracle that we recognize ourselves! It's not called "the change" for nothing!

I'm certain post-menopausal life has an upside. There is freedom in knowing I don't have to worry about an unplanned pregnancy! There is delight in never having an "unexpected visit from Aunt Flo."

Still, we can expect to become forgetful. As we age, men and women will lose muscle and tone, and it is more difficult to get or stay fit.

For women, those issues are compounded with this evolutionary process that changes us at our core. And (let me make a social generalization here) because it falls under "women's issues," it's rarely spoken of in public.

Miraculously, most women can navigate this process with humor and the help of medical professionals. There is no need to go it alone, and if you find it becoming unmanageable, talking with your doctor is always a good idea! There are medications and organic treatments to help balance the ebbs and flows of hormonal imbalances.

I'm looking at menopause as another remarkable part of

the journey that is the human experience, and I believe there is freedom in not only surviving but embracing this next chapter. All kidding aside, there is no arguing that this life journey is fascinating and ever changing and I do look forward to whatever is coming up ahead.

I'm banking on more "m's" like magical and marvelous and many more years of making memories.

"N" is for Neck

It was the late Nora Ephron who penned the tome, "I Feel Bad About My Neck", which is a hilarious take on getting older, and the things that happen to our bodies.

I was just 18 years old the first time a friend brought up the fact that we were aging. She came into our apartment, arms full of groceries and said, "Have you noticed how old my hands look?"

I did not think they looked old at all, but ever since, every now and again, while driving or washing dishes or putting on gloves, I would take a pause and give my hands a good long look. Do they look older?

Until recently I would have denied any signs of wear, but the invention of the high-speed air hand dryers makes it impossible to ignore. For those who have yet to use one of these remarkable inventions, the apparatus is mounted on a wall with wide slots. The idea is to insert your hands into the wide slots, which triggers a force of air meant to dry your hands in a timely fashion. It's a step up from those old-fashioned air dryers that require correct hand placement for the optimum effect. These newly fangled driers are ferocious and efficient. Unfortunately, the force of the wind actually causes the too loose skin on the back of my hands to slide back and forth. It kind of reminds me of the way it feels to put your face out a car window! I had no idea the skin on my hands was so loose, but there's no denying it now!

My friends and I were asked for identification before being allowed entrance into a 21 and older club. We were shocked and flattered. Apparently, they were not taking any chances. "Just look at my hands," one friend exclaimed. "That's what I do. No need to look at our faces, if you are wondering if we are old enough, the hands are a dead giveaway."

I looked down and realized my skin is thinning, my veins are more prominent, and the back of my hands have more "freckles" than a red headed stepchild.

Okay, so my hands are showing wear. I have written about this before. But the pace of the aging process is astonishing. One day I was thinking, "not bad," and the next it was, "Holy crap, when did that happen?"

In truth, it's not just my hands showing signs of wear. Though I do not officially advance in age for another few months, my body is not waiting for it to be sanctioned.

I took inventory of some other areas and felt completely betrayed.

As the puffiness, dark circles and slack eye lids clearly illustrate, I have never used fillers or Botox or surgery to reduce wrinkles. I think my face is fine, overall, but there is no denying the neck.

Recently, sometime in the night, while I slept somewhat fitfully, a part of my chin slid off my face and landed on my neck! I did not realize it until I caught a side glance in the mirror. I quickly took my wrinkled, dried-out digits and tried pulling my face back up where it belonged, but to no avail. All that slack skin sliding has turned it into something else entirely. I can see the possibility of a future resemblance to a turkey or other slack-jawed bird in profile. I now compare my neck to an elephant's foot. Google the image for yourself and you will see what I mean. There are deep creases that defy direction and extra skin with no place to go.

The only smooth parts are those that I can only assume used to be my chin! That theory was cemented with the discovery of a hair about 3 inches long, protruding from my collar! Now how did that happen? And how did the hair grow so long undetected? I'm certain the pace of hair growth has slowed considerably over the years, maybe while it was still part of my face, it was near my ear, and I just couldn't see it!

Gravity also wreaks havoc on the aging body. I have already written about the depressing war my bosom is losing to the force. A complete surrender is imminent. I am looking into a pulley system to get through the next decade.

I could continue, moving my way south, but that is not the point, "cankles" be damned! Suffice it to say I reluctantly accept the unavoidable demise of the condition of the human body.

When did the skin become so loose? So thin? So, lined? And I must admit, the newly discovered "freckles" may be something else. Whoever coined the term "age spots" knew of what they spoke.

This is not the first time I have noticed the aging process taking over, but I guess I thought the overall progression would be more of a glacial pace. Instead, it seems to be picking up speed—more like running down the proverbial hill I recently ascended. (Over the hill? What hill? I didn't see any hill! So, the saying goes!)

And then there are, of course, the noises that escape with each effort. The groans and moans and sighs that accompany generally any exertion is a mini symphony. So much for peace and quiet.

Regardless, I have always known gravity would play a role in body part relocation. I had heard the tales of sagging this and drooping that. Still, I was unprepared for the sheer volume vying for closer proximity to my feet than the place of origin. And since some of those parts are not easily seen, the drop has literally snuck up on me.

Of course, I realize physical changes are part of the aging process. Crow's feet, laugh lines, wrinkles, folds, and furrows—they are all signs of life lived. Along with hair that is thinning and turning grey and legs that no longer need see the light of day, I have accepted it all as inevitable. On my best days, I see it as the reward for having made it this far.

What I will continue to resist, however, are the aches and pains that seem to be ever increasing and come on for no reason whatsoever. I find myself hobbling down the hall each morning as I encourage my ankles to loosen up and find their rhythm.

A daily walk begins with a knee that is not at all certain it remembers just how to bend and straighten and comes with a little creak each time I extend it. Even after an hour of movement, my body protests as I bend to pick up the daily newspaper that is faithfully delivered to the end of my driveway.

When did bending over become a three-part strategy? Step 1: Assess the situation – could I get away with a squat or a kneel? Step 2: Take a deep breath in. Step 3: Breathe out and fold!

People tell me to stretch. I know all about stretching. I stretch my arm to the medicine cabinet and reach for the pain reliever on a pretty regular basis.

I look upon the next cold season and think of all the lore around stiff joints and brittle bones. I consider myself too young to be concerned with breaking a hip, but I have finally given up the idea of snowboarding or skiing as a form of winter recreation and exercise. I don't want to risk it.

I think of my poor knees, my ankles, my aching back. I don't like it. I barely recognize this kind of thinking. My intent was to be forever young.

I try to stay healthy and keep up a pretty active social life. My body is growing older, but I am refusing to grow up. I will work on the side of me that is not defined by unwanted wrinkles and inflexible joints.

As writer William W. Purkey suggested, "Sing like no one is listening. Love like you've never been hurt. Dance like nobody's watching and live like it is heaven on earth."

I'm willing to stick my neck out and say it may be a puddle of skin starting at my jawline and resting on my shoulder blades, but it is all mine! Sure, there are modern procedures that could put it all back where it began. It could use a lift. I have pondered spending the money, but the effort seems ultimately futile. A personal decision for sure, but I will accept what is coming as naturally as possible. I believe accepting the process with grace is as valid a choice as those who fight back with injections and surgery.

As with Nora, I do feel bad about my neck. I also feel bad about all the other sagging and aching parts. There is is another saying, "If I had known I was going to live this long, I would have taken better care of myself."

"O" is for Old

Today is my husband's birthday. I would not be so brash as to say exactly how old he is, but I will say I have had a certain Beatles song running through my head for weeks. You know the one. "Will still need me? Will you still feed me when I'm …"?

When I first wrote this five years ago, I had known this man for nearly a quarter of a century. It has been a remarkable, long, and winding road, to continue quoting from the Fab Four. I find one of the most interesting parts of our journey to be the process of aging.

I don't think either of us could have imagined the changes that would take place in our lives as the children grew up and our days moved away from back-to-school nights and summer vacations and into the hope of an empty nest with retirement coming into view.

I know neither of us were prepared for the physical changes our bodies would undergo as we moved out of middle age and into whatever age this might be. We are still active and neither of us really think of ourselves as old, but we tend to disagree about what old means.

We recently saw news of the death of a famous actor and, as is often the case, our conversation went something like this:

Me: Honey, (name of famous actor) died.
Him: How old was he?
Me: 85.

Him: He was a young man.
Me: No, honey, he was old.
Him: 85 is not that old.
Me: Yes. It is.
Him: No. It's not.
Me: Yes. It is. (Name of another actor who also died) was relatively young (at 52). That other guy was old.
Him: Not today. People live to be 100.
Me: That may be true, but they are old.

So maybe we are not so "old," but we are most definitely no longer young. It's one of those things that just sort of creeped up when we weren't paying attention. We often have discussions on the topic. We discuss failing eyesight, stiff joints, backaches, hair that has turned gray or completely abandoned its post, necks that have become slack and spots on our skin.

And we are most definitely slowing down. I must admit that change is not all bad.

Slowing down allows us to appreciate each day a bit more. We have a better sense of what is important and of course, we now have all that wisdom that has come with living a long-ish life.

However, my husband finds aging an especially egregious process and is fighting the good fight to thwart it at every turn. But, despite the effort, there are some obvious signs that time is marching on. I see the passion in him that was once a blazing bonfire, now more akin to a controlled burn. His need to conquer the world has been replaced with a bit of complacency. He does not find many issues worth fighting over. I am working on doing the same. But then, I am younger than him!

Ultimately, I think what we fear most of all—beyond a

body that does not respond as it once did or a mind that is not as sharp as it once was—is the fear of being irrelevant. We do not want to be ineffective or without purpose. A friend recently said, "Of all the "ism's," ageism is the worst." I am not sure it is the worst, but it certainly ranks high on the list. The tendency to cast aside, rather than revere our elders is one of our biggest societal failures.

Though that is up for debate. Let me clarify to say we should revere our elders who still maintain their faculties. Maybe imparting their hard-earned wisdom as advisors to world leaders versus doing the actual leading.

I understand this now that I am "of a certain age."

I give my spouse a hard time, but in truth, I admire him. I admire the fight. He has been coaching football for as long as I have known him. He continues to make an impact on the lives of those kids, with purpose and relevance.

And, as I have mentioned, he is in great shape, and he works hard at it. He watches what he eats and balances any indulgences in his diet with an extra mile on the trail or with a few extra holes on the golf course. He may well live to be 100. He explained that he is simply unwilling to give in to the process. Each time he is forced to accept that he simply cannot do something due to his age, he balks. He is no longer running marathons in under four hours. He moves slower in the morning. His back and his knees scream in protest at the constant workouts. He presses on. He simply refuses to give in.

I am certain I am not that kind of girl. I am more inclined to let the chips fall where they may, and I can only hope I will be able to keep up with him. I am fortunate to be several years younger, but I am not sure that will work to my advantage.

Another lap around the sun is coming up for me and I think of the Aerosmith lyrics, "Every time that I look in the mirror. All these lines in my face keep getting clearer. The past is gone. It went by like dusk to dawn…" Such profound musings from a then teenage Steven Tyler, who probably had a bigger issue with acne than wrinkles when he penned that tune. I love every lyric in that song and find them insightful and accurate.

Dream on.

With another birthday imminent, I see the lines in my face joined by bags under my eyes and skin slinking down my arms and wonder where did all the time go? When did these wrinkles become permanent fixtures? What happened to bouncing back? I can attribute specific areas to events, children, or work-related issues. "See that one right there? It appeared within days of my kid moving abroad for the first time. And this one, when I decided to work for a crazy person. And that one appeared right after a family reunion. Need I say more?"

On a positive note, there are very few people I know who are aging the same way our grandparents, or even our parents, aged. It could be worse! We look so much better than our predecessors.

I was looking at a photo of my mother that was taken in 1988. She looks, well, elderly. She has white hair and age spots, and her frame is bending slightly. She is also, in that photo, the same age I will be in a week.

I do not mean to boast, but there is no way I look that old! Of course, her life and my life were quite different. She was born during the depression. She gave birth to seven children! Certainly, I should cut her some slack! In many ways, times have changed. Modern conveniences make for an easier existence. I understand that. Though an argument could be made that the source of stress has merely shifted.

At any rate, I am jumping on the anti-shame about aging train. We need a societal shift, especially for women. A case in point followed a Grammy Awards broadcast. The media was all abuzz about how Madonna looked (which was, admittedly, shocking) with what appears to be plastic surgery gone wrong, while there was hardly a whisper over Smokey Robinson's appearance. The octogenarian did not appear to be sporting any original parts, with a face so tight it is still possible to trace the tracks of his tears.

I feel bad for those compelled to fight so hard against aging. It takes a ton of time, effort, and money to combat the inevitable changing body. I am not talking about diet or exercise. I am talking about injections and lotions and potions and surgery. I am not talking about procedures or parts replacements that improve the quality of your life. I am talking about the drastic measures taken to alter the appearance of years of living.

Sure, I am guilty of hiding the persistent grey hair, so maybe I am being a little hypocritical, but aside from this one indulgence, I say, "Bring it on." I have lived a good life full of bad decisions, and many of those poor choices are now reflected in my mirror.

Certainly, there is plenty to complain about. Each morning is a revelation as I inventory what parts are still working properly versus what muscle or joint is clamoring for attention. A couple of weeks ago, I lifted a half a case— a mere five reams of paper—from the back of an office supply store to the counter and then to my vehicle. The next day I felt like I had gone five rounds in a boxing ring. My muscles ached. I was sure I pinched a nerve! It took days for me to recover. Days.

It turns out all those years I spent at the gym strength training and stretching were of no long-lasting benefit. The human body simply does not store fitness. In the realm of use it or lose it, it has all been lost. Time to begin again.

Because, while I am not pro cosmetic alteration, I am pro doing what I can to prolong a good life.

The truth is it is a privilege to grow old! The list of those I knew who did not get to have this experience has grown far too long for me to spend too much time complaining. Instead, I am going to focus on embracing what is left of this journey. I am committing to doing what it takes to live a good life, despite the rebelling vessel that carries me through each day.

Over the past year I gave my livelihood top billing over my life. The daily walk with my girlfriend became optional and then all but stopped. Taking time to exercise simply felt like one more thing I just didn't have time to do. It is time to renew the ritual.

I do spend some time in gratitude each morning. I journal. I meditate, often poorly, but I do meditate. (We can talk about monkey brain at another time). I plan to add some daily stretching, and at some point, give those pathetic muscles a chance to regain their sense of pride. It's time to say so long to saggy and hello to strong. It doesn't take much, but it does take a regular commitment. For all I have put this body through, it's the least I can do.

None of us know how long we will be in this realm and the challenge is to embrace each day. Find the things that bring happiness and do those things as often as possible. Because you just never know (to finish off the Aerosmith reference) "maybe tomorrow the good Lord will take you away."

Whenever that day comes for me, I plan to have a smile on this wrinkled, saggy, baggy face. I say, "Let It Be"!

"P" is for Pain

So much pain as we age—physical and mental! I feel all the painful parts that make up me these days: back pain, knee pain, ankle pain, neck pain, feet pain, pain from loss, pain from play. Any part I use today will be talking to me about it later or certainly in the morning.

My husband has been remodeling our house. It's a 45-year-old log home built from a pre-designed kit where all the materials you need to build the home are delivered, presumably with instructions. The original owner was an artist, not a contractor, and it shows. The result is a high maintenance home that had almost no maintenance for over 20 years. It seems the builder may have missed the steps on sealing and treatment to the wood that would keep it safe from decay. A good number of the pressure treated built-to-last logs have rotted to the core in just a couple of decades.

Regardless of the reason, we must replace the logs. And to be clear, by "we," I mean my husband.

Hubby was, at one point in his career, a licensed contractor. He retired a few years ago from another career, so once he had the time, his job became remodeling the homestead, or more accurately, rebuilding the house. It has turned out to be a full-time gig with no end in sight.

But I helped! I watched him slog up and down the ladder, tearing out the existing logs and replacing the house front with traditional siding. He's done 100 percent of the heavy lifting, cutting, framing, nailing, and precariously lifting the sheets of plywood up the ladder, using engineering creativity to nail them into place. During the entire process, he asked me to help four times—basically to hold a sheet of plywood in place after he lifted it over his head. My job was to use a clamp to secure the piece so he could nail it to the frame. The last of the four pieces required me to squat for about 10 seconds, maybe less, but it was awkward, and I held the stance until he shimmied it just so and I secured the clamp. Voile la!

However, the next day, I could barely stand. My quads screamed in protest! What had I done? A measly half squat for less than a count to ten? Oh, this getting old thing is a thing!

As we age, muscle strength is vitally important. I was told we lose a certain percentage of strength each year after age 40, which is why the general over 60 population tends to be weak.

I have learned there is no banking fitness. It's not a savings account we can draw from—use it or lose it is the real deal. Muscle tone fades away as quickly as the setting sun, and when we try to do any of those things we used to do, our body is quick to let us know what is and what in not okay.

Yesterday, I bent over to pick a bed pillow off the floor as I made the bed, and I felt some protest at the base of my spine. Suddenly, I could not stand up. I injured myself by picking up a pillow!

Physical pain is an accepted part of the aging process for most everyone I know who has outlived their mileage warranty. I am not fighting it.

Emotional pain is harder to deal with, at least for me.

The pain of losing those we love or having relationships turn sour and come to an unexpected end is much harder to accept and treat. The older I get, the more common this experience, yet the tools used to withstand it are elusive. Grief counseling might be helpful and there are countless books on the subject. The process is just that, a process. Keeping those we lost alive with memories is about as good as it gets, which feels woefully inadequate. This pain lingers.

When I hurt my back, I knew what to do. When the pain is physical, I can make myself a morning cocktail of coffee and ibuprofen, followed by the main course of heating pad and staying horizontal for most of the morning.

Emotional pain is different. There is no magic pill. Time is said to ease the pain. Time will tell.

In either case, going slow appears to be the best course of action. We can't rush through rehabilitating tweaked muscles and that includes a broken heart.

"Q" is for Quinquagenarian

From the Latin word quīnquāgēnārius, which means "containing fifty". Those fifty somethings just cannot know what is coming—so smug, so secure, so naïve! I hear them, thinking they see the light, as they notice a slower pace, or mention a little ache here and there, but, brothers and sisters, I am here to tell you, there is a train up ahead!

‣ In my 50's, I began the long and lengthy menopause journey but really did not understand the decades stretched road on which I was embarking. I thought I was going to float on through. In fact, the theme for my birthday that year was "cruising into 50"—literally. I got a group of friends together and we set sail across the water on a giant ship. I even had t-shirts made to commemorate the journey. A dozen of us, most near age 50, spent a week in celebration, eating and drinking with abandon. As my husband says, "We stepped on the ship and didn't take a sober breath until we landed back home."

It was a special gathering with some of my longest relationships, including a girlfriend I met in 5th grade, and it included my two newest friends who were amid a twelve month experiment they called "a year without a man." They were nine months into a celibate and relationship free year. The group also included my best friends from my youth, my husband's bestie, and his wife.

Completing the party were a few former classmates from

high school who said "yes" when I threw it out to my graduating class, since we were mostly all hitting 50 that year.

It was an interesting mix of people who represented many aspects of my life: childhood friends, child rearing era friends, long lost and new friends, all coming together. My momentary concern of whether everyone would get along was unfounded as the camaraderie was instant and organic with lots of pool time, imbibing, and adventure.

At 50, I ziplined for the first time, and took one scary ride down the ship's massive water slide. It may have been built for a smaller or at least lighter person than the pounds I was carrying at the time—I came down that thing with Olympic medal winning luge speed and there are photos of a sideways dismount that would have easily received a disqualification for going out of bounds as my hips ricocheted out of the chute. I would have likely earned a judges' scale 1.5 on the dismount.

We wandered through cities and took different excursions. I lost my husband for a bit after he ventured solo into the heart of a neighborhood on one of the stops in Mexico, finding a front yard barbeque and fifty cent cans of beers, while others in our group opted for a beach experience.

The first night on the ship I was awakened to what I thought was the sound of a cat. My first thought was to wonder how someone managed to sneak a cat onboard. Eventually, I recognized the noise as not from a feline, but rather the noise of a rambunctious couple a few suites down who were copulating. I had time to figure it out because it happened repeatedly throughout the cruise! This insatiable couple was booked amid our group—sandwiched between the women who were nine months into their celibacy journey and the couple who were unknowingly enjoying their last decade together before cancer put an end to the relationship.

The celibate women, at first jealous, became annoyed and agitated as the sex went on morning, noon, and night. At one point, one of the pair began echoing the noises emitting from the open balcony door. Ah "ah" Oh "oh" and on it went.

The men in our group took on a more competitive approach, trying to seduce their wives with the same vigor, but to no avail. At a certain point, there was no keeping up in repetition or duration!

It turned out the loud and prolific mystery couple had only been dating a few months and 50 was nowhere in their purview. "No wonder," one of our cruise mates exclaimed. "Hang another decade or two on them. Just wait until they are 50 and see how many times a day, they are doing the horizontal bop!" And now I think, oh, how naïve we all were.

For those lucky enough to have moved forward to 60 and 60 plus, we can now see clearly that the quinquagenarian was having a delightful time. The kids were grown and beginning to leave the roost. Retirement was in sight. Our bodies were still cooperating. The fifties were a sweet spot. I'm not talking about Happy Days 50's sweet. I'm talking about the "Greased Lightening" Thunderbird sweet, when most of our parts were still in working order, sex was still in drive, the body and engine were still under a service contract.

We really were cruising through life. We had no way of knowing that a giant iceberg lay just around the corner!

"R" is for Relative

Life is full of choices. You can pick your friends. You can pick your career. You can pick your place of residence, but you cannot pick your family—at least not your family of origin.

Relatively speaking, I grew up with a plethora of siblings, cousins, aunts, and uncles, and what a wacky bunch. Of course, I did not understand that we were a bunch of poor, white folk. Not a lot of higher education in the group, and the houses we visited, when we visited those relatives, were a lifetime away from those depicted on television. At one point my family owned enough single-wides to open our own park.

I spent some overnight visits with one aunt and uncle who in my memory (and maybe that is simply the perspective of a child) had a huge house, though there was not a drop of paint still visible on the exterior. There we (my cousins and I) would climb into bed in an attic bedroom while the scurry of rodents lulled us into slumber. Most of our family reunions took place there. I am guessing because the house, though dilapidated, by our family standard, was enormous.

At mealtime, we would wait for the "all clear" before diving into a potluck of assorted salads and casseroles placed on a long table in a covered porch. The "all clear" to dig in came after one or more of the adults waved their arms across the dishes to disrupt the blanket of flies that had stopped to graze. It was as natural a part of my upbringing before summer meals as saying grace might be for others.

Until I was out in the world, I didn't realize this was not how everyone was living. I had no idea the level of poverty I got my start in, and that it was not how everyone else was being raised.

As a positive, I can say I rarely get sick and attribute my hearty immune system to the years spent in the dirt and muck of lack.

Now I see that pay off as I age and look to genetics to realize my lineage includes some hearty souls. Though none of my grandparents, aunts, uncles, or parents made it 100 years on this planet, they were all pretty active until their end.

As previously mentioned, the gene pool comes with a little heart disease, some diabetes, a smattering of Alzheimer's—but most were living vibrantly on their own through their mid-80's. I hope to be at least among their ranks, also living vibrantly into my 80's, but hopefully beyond them, into my 90's with a sound mind, body, and spirit.

These days my fear is not so much ailments as it is outliving the money. Modern medicine and medical advancements keep coming, extending the average life span, which is great news in many respects, but I am not sure my husband and I will be able to afford it. Our financial advisor has shown projections with us living into our 90's and there is a shortfall.

Even without any major medical issues, how are we

expected to pay for all this living we have ahead of us? Good health and good living are our goals, and I want to spend it adventuring. Sometimes I think I'll be the old lady on the cruise ship, booking month long excursions to all parts of the globe— cheaper than assisted living, I hear!

Other times that exploration might take place in a recliner if the form of a good book. Some of my favorite adventures have been supplied by great writers.

A long life could mean a long retirement. As the youngest of seven children, I look to my older siblings to see how they are doing it, and I am a bit concerned. They appear to be retired to living on conservative paths—not a lot of travel, two international journeys between them. It appears the "wanderlust" gene was saved for me!

I do hear about occasional plans for a few days at the beach or a weekend gambling in Sin City. Once, my brother and sister-in-law spent a few weeks travelling coast to coast, which was a grand adventure for them and afforded me time to show off my community, when a leg of their journey brought them to my driveway. Some good memories, there!

Mostly, they have not ventured to many places beyond our hometown, or much past the homes they settled into after finding a spouse—the desert for one, the flat lands in a fly over state for another. My siblings simply do not appear to be all that adventurous. They are living in the day-to-day existence of long marriages, with their families raised, and are deeply rooted. That is another type of venture altogether.

Maybe they are simply trying to make sure they don't outlive their money as well!

While it is really none of my business, I find myself

unsettled with their choices to "stay put", while there is still so much left to explore and to do. In my opinion, many of my relatives appear to be relatively content, but have let go of their dreams and have forgotten the aspirations of their younger selves. As I age, I see how easy it can be for some people to stop dreaming, stop planning, and instead get up each day only to watch the sun travel across the sky from the same vantage point, as one day turns into the next.

People who know me will scoff at me and my judgements. I have travelled but not nearly enough. Mostly, I work. I work a lot. The beauty comes when my work requires travel and I'm able to tack a day or two to the trip to actually enjoy the places when the work is finished.

My husband has relatives who live closer to a century and he's spending his days fighting the call of age. As I have mentioned several times at this point, he's busy running, bike riding, stretching, lifting, monitoring food and diet, all in the fight against getting old, but he let his passport expire and resisted getting it renewed. Only the threat of leaving the country without him finally got him to do it!! He appears content to spend his days in routine—hours spent each day completing the "to do's"—but to be clear, not the "honey-do's".

Days can easily fill up with the "have to's" and not the "want to's." But happiness is a state of mind, and age is just a number. I think curiosity keeps us alive. Having something to look forward to has been proven to be good for us. Studies have shown the planning of an event can be as beneficial as the actual doing. To that end, I call on each of us to get a bucket and make a list. Commit to crossing one item off each year, if not more frequently.

For some, that may be ambitious items like visiting every national park or hiking the Appalachian trail. For others, it may be as simple as getting the house painted or putting screens on the doors to keep the flies out. Our bodies come with a limit and how we use it usually can help or hinder the process.

Our lineage can be a factor in our longevity but so can a good diet and exercise plan. My idea of what a good life looks like seems to be very different from other family members. I believe aging is a privilege and I don't want to waste a minute, but that is my take. Who am I to judge? Old age is a state of being and of being at choice—squander it or embrace it.

My hope is to stop working while I am healthy enough to adventure, or that my work and my adventures will coexist. Now that is a retirement plan, I can get behind!

It is not up to me to judge – though clearly, I do. What is important is to spend these days doing what feels good and what feels good to me is likely different from what feels good to you.

It's all relative.

"S" is for Sleep

It's 3:30 in the morning and I am awake. After going to bed at a reasonable time in the late evening and sleeping for a bit, I have been awake for a couple of hours.

I tend to spend some time reading before turning off the light and drifting off to slumber. I aim for seven to eight hours of sleep a night. However, lately, my night of rest has suffered repeated interruption. For whatever reason, I have found myself waking sometime between 1 a.m. and 4 a.m. and staying awake for a several hours.

Lying in bed, I'm at first hopeful that I will fall back to sleep and reconnect with the lingering memory of the dream I was having. But soon, it becomes obvious sleep will elude me. I find myself tossing, readjusting my pillow, and listening to my mind as it wanders from topic to topic. I replay the day's events. I ponder the future. I revisit conversations with friends and acquaintances. I plan future travel. I think about the kids. I think about my "to do" list.

I send good thoughts and blessings to family members. I count my breaths. I count sheep. I sing "99 bottles of beer on the wall" in my head. I wonder who else might be awake, and wish I knew who they were so we could chat. I contemplate giving up and getting up. I toss and turn some more. I elbow my husband in the ribs for breathing wrong.

I write stories in my head. I think of things I meant to do that I haven't done. I throw the covers off as I am suddenly extremely warm. I think about places I want to go and things I want to do. I retrieve the covers and turn again as I am suddenly a bit chilly. I get up and drink a glass of water. I use the bathroom. I let the cat out. I return to bed. I beg for sleep. I try not to resent the rhythmic mostly soft snoring of my obviously deeply sleeping husband. I look at the clock and start doing the math: "If I get to sleep within the next five minutes, I can still get 'x' number of hours of rest." I quiet my brain and eventually, I drift off into slumber.

When my alarm sounds a few hours (or minutes) later, I am in a deep sleep and can barely find my way to the shower. Exhausted.

You get the picture. I am quite clear that I am not alone. I am, by nature, a night owl. I love to stay up late, and I love to sleep in.

Life does not always allow for my ideal schedule, so I adjust, but I am in awe and mystified by those who purposely get up and start their day at 5 a.m. I know I can do so; I did it for years when it was a work requirement. But I would never choose it. As I age, I am told that may change.

I am on the upper end of late middle to early old age. As my physiology changes, I am adjusting. I am in the throes of it. Naively, I thought I was pretty much through the changes my body had in store, and I thought I had come through them relatively unscathed. I have heard horror stories. I expected a little bit of crazy or mood swings, as the more polite among us describe it. I was looking forward to hot flashes—I hate being cold, so a night sweat or two did not sound so bad.

About a year ago, I naively thought I was done. I was incorrect. I did a quick Google search to see what some of the common symptoms are for this next chapter of life and found a list of the top 34 most common. THIRTY-FOUR. I perused the list and there it was—right there between mood swings, hot flashes, weight gain and night sweats: sleeping disorders.

So that's it. It's not too much caffeine, worry, stress, the full moon, or any of the other possibilities I have played out in my non-sleeping brain. It's simply a symptom of where I am biologically. It could even be deemed normal, given my age. Oh boy. Lucky me.

Knowing the probable cause does not really help with day-to-day function, but it does give me a little peace of mind. I am confident now that it is not chronic. This, too, shall pass.

In the meantime, I will spend my wee-hour wakefulness as productively as possible. And that being said, it's now time to try to get some sleep.

"T" is for Technology

I've become that lady: the one who can't keep up. Technology is not my friend. I thought it was. In the way back times, like in the early 1970's, I was all about it! I was thrilled when I was replaced as the family channel changer. Our first remote control was a box that was attached to the television with a long cord. We'd come a long way from aluminum foil on a rabbit ear antenna, trying to watch a show on one of the three available networks or PBS, in black and white. There we were, living the dream in living color!

Next up came the Beta vs VHS recorders where we could watch movies, straight from the big screen to the comfort of our own home. Programming that machine was the next task given to the children. While my parents could not quite master the directions, my siblings and I tackled the instruction manual with fervor and even learned to set the time correctly. Our parents were just not able to win the man versus machine battle. Oh, how feeble I thought they must be!

Now, some 50 years later, technology and time took on warp speed. Not only computers, software and all that goes with it, but social platforms like Instagram and Tik Toc and

Snapchat, and who knows what else is being rolled out hourly. How is anyone keeping up? There is probably an app for that but learning the app and using the app before a new, better, faster, never easier app, replaces the one I've most recently mastered is a lesson in futility.

Technology, like time, please, I am begging. Slow down! Time, which waits for no one, is speeding by and not only is technology progressing at a pace that is nearly impossible to keep pace with, it has also become something we have to find our way through. Unlike the Beta machine my stepfather brought into our home (yes, he backed the wrong horse), it is nearly impossible to function in this world without embracing our computerized existence.

Oh, technology! I feel forsaken.

Recently I was out of town, working on the laptop I purchased a mere four months before, when things turned sour. "Do you smell that," a coworker asked? "It smells electrical," I said and literally got down on my hands and knees to sniff around the power strip. We both got up and moved away from the table in search of the source of the odor when I realized my computer screen was black. I pushed the space bar thinking maybe it had timed out, only to realize the smell was emitting from the back of my PC. My computer was fried. My ability to work, dead in the water.

Whyyyyyyyyyy?

I was able to borrow a "spare" system and, having learned my lesson a few short months before after my previous computer was stolen, now had much of my work accessible "in the cloud" for which I am most grateful but in reality, do not clearly understand.

They Aren't Even Trying Anymore

I sent a missive to the local computer guru in town and was quickly directed to contact the manufacturer. The long story is I am now working on a "loaner" from this kind business owner and my computer is travelling across America for repair or replacement. It could be a couple of weeks, and I am limping along, trying to find documents and programs as I work in what feels like outer space.

To add to my woes, my printer stopped functioning properly. It prints but it won't feed, so the paper gets jammed up. It is quite frustrating and really testing my ability to get things done.

When I complained to my friends (and anyone who would listen), a surprising number of people gave me feedback that went something along the lines of, "Well, you know six of the planets are aligned in retrograde and we are close to Gemini moving into Pluto and Saturn is coming close to Uranus and when Jupiter aligns with Mars and enters Gemini, it's no wonder you are having to do everything twice!" (This is not a direct or accurate quote.) Are we living in the days of Galileo? We are a long way from two lenses and a tube to help us navigate the planet, though that may have been the rudimentary technology of the time. I can hear my kids, "Ma, you have the wrong end of the tube pointing at the sky. Try the other end..."

At any rate, I am not convinced the planetary alignments are the cause of my technology woes but do know my dependence on technology is alarming. Our world runs on the web! We are all incredibly dependent and at the mercy of electronic communication networks. It's frightening and it all happened so quickly, it is no wonder many of us struggle to keep up.

It has not been all that long ago that systems changed from manual to computerized and there is no way to go back. I was working at IBM in Endicott, New York, in the 1970's when we used a desktop typewriter that stored everything typed and allowed the operator to recall and revise previously typed material on a magnetic card. It was magic beyond my scope of understanding! There was also the IBM Selectric, with little balls that could be interchanged for different fonts and it utilized automatic correcting tape to fix errors. A secretary's dream come true. How could it get any better than that?

I grew up with manual bookkeeping where we used large ledgers and hand wrote all transactions, balancing debits and credits using our math skills and 10-key systems.

I worked in a grocery store where we punched in the amounts of products into registers and counted change back, which we calculated in our heads!

I realize I sound prehistoric. I wasn't quite chiseling rock before these marvels came into being but given the lightning speed in which the way we work has changed, maybe I am ancient.

Suffering through two computer losses in just a few months has illuminated my dependency on what was supposed to help us work smarter and not harder. Remember the idea of a paperless society? Remember how we were supposed to be able to work less since the systems were so efficient? We'd all be able to complete daily tasks in minutes instead of hours with nothing but free time on our hands! Remember how our quality of life was going to improve immensely? What happened?

We work and we work. We never really complete our tasks, as they pile up higher and higher. I find myself responding to emails (from my phone) at all hours and all days of the week. It is incredibly difficult for me to unplug.

They Aren't Even Trying Anymore

Last weekend I went to see a comedian perform in Sacramento with a group of friends. Our phones, which held our tickets were scanned, and then, along with our "smart" watches were placed in a pouch that was magnetically sealed and we were not able to retrieve the devices from the pouch until we left the venue.

For nearly two hours I was without the ability to connect with the outside world. I did not know what time it was. I was incredibly uncomfortable! What if there was an emergency? What if my husband or children needed to get in touch with me? What if?

I am here to admit to my addiction to technology. I am almost never without my phone. I use my debit and credit cards to track my spending. I wear a device that tracks my activities and calories. I will never be lost, as I use GPS navigation wherever I go.

It didn't take long for me to transition from manual to cyber systems. The big question is what happens when the system fails? Have you been at the grocery store or the bank or a restaurant when the power has gone off? I was the recipient of a free dinner under those circumstances because the server was simply at a loss – they couldn't bring up my bill or calculate the cost and I wasn't carrying any cash. I have been forced to leave groceries at the checkout for similar reasons and have thus decided storing some cash at an undisclosed location is not the worst idea, though if the cyber system does suffer a fatal crash, would cash still have value? Something else to ponder!

I don't have the answer, but I believe as long as the worldwide web keeps spinning, and the planets continue in their orbit, and that nice manufacturer sends back my laptop in working order, I will be fine. This time.

In this new world, technology is clearly the winner of the popularity contest.

Everything will be better once we become friends.

"U" is for Un

Understanding… unhappy… unfortunate … underwhelmed… unmotivated … – yes! That is how my brain is working these days. It's a do-nothing day, grey and cold and drizzling outside. I literally stayed in bed all morning playing word games on my phone and tackling The Morning Brew crossword puzzle. I like The Morning Brew—a concise romp through world finance and news with a bit of tongue and cheek humor and not too many shameless plugs from sponsors. And, not every day, but many days, it includes a crossword puzzle I'm able to decipher, while not necessarily to completion, at least complete enough to feel a tiny bit of accomplishment.

I have never thought myself to be very good at crossword puzzles, but they remind me of my mother who used to play and complete them, on a fairly frequent basis. My brain just doesn't or didn't work that way. An eight-letter word for contrary? I don't know. Isn't contrary an eight-letter word? Why do we need another one? I totally made that up. If there is another eight-letter word with the same meaning, it is not coming to me now. No, crossword puzzles are a challenge for the way this brain works, but give me a good word search and I'll be entertained for days.

My fondness for word search probably goes back to picture search pages in those old Highlight Magazines often found on a table in the waiting room on those rare occasions my mom and I would be visiting the doctor's office. Only now do I wonder if that means we were visiting a pediatrician— unlikely (another "u" word)—more likely, it was family practice.

In those days, those days being the 1960's, I was too young to be left to my own devices. If my mom had any appointments on her day off, I would be in tow. Visiting the doctor would mean bringing me along and keeping me happily occupied with the picture search page, ruined only when some selfish patient, prior to my arrival, had the audacity to circle the hidden objects—spoiler! The only worse crime was to find the page had been torn from the magazine completely—just gone! Incredibly disappointing to me and utterly (there's that "u" again) selfish! I will never grasp that kind of thinking or behavior.

It's been a long time since I thought about those desecrated magazine picture puzzles. Giving the benefit of the doubt to the offenders, maybe they just weren't thinking about the next kid! Nah, that was just rude!

We are all unique beings with our own understanding of acceptable behavior. But as I age, I find myself lacking patience for the selfish. We're all just trying to live our best life, searching for our own purpose and sense of what brings each of us joy. Can we do that without causing harm?

When the pandemic hit in 2020, the initial sense was we were all in it together and people came together in support of humanity—neighbors and strangers alike. We began seeing signs that "we are all in the same boat," but quickly, (too quickly) it became evident that we were not all in the same boat, but more accurately, in the same storm. As the storm raged on, there were some people in yachts and others in cruisers, some sailing, and others in canoes, some in rafts and many others hanging onto what debris happened to float by. That translates to the lives we were living. For those with a plethora of resources and unlimited finances, only the limitations of border crossing hampered their existence. Others hung on by a thread, relying on subsidies, the kindness of strangers, and government policies. And there were those in the middle, who prospered in the new world. They looked at what they were doing and changed what did not work.

A couple of my offspring had a relatively good pandemic, getting out of the service industry, using stimulus checks to pay off debt, taking time to learn new skills, vying to work their way up to a bigger boat.

I took the time to look at my priorities and options. I got in touch with people I cared about and worked to heal estrangements—sometimes successfully, but not always.

Being of a certain age did give me perspective and an understanding that more of my time has already been spent on Earth in this human form than the time that is still ahead.

What I understand above all else is that when I no longer recognize my loved ones, should it come to that, I will be okay making my exit. I do not want to live in that place. I know people say I won't know I am in that place, but I think, on some level, I will know. And given my family history, a UTI is bound to be part of that long goodbye—have you ever had one of those? The worst! I'm not unique. I understand—all the "u" words that come to mind are valid, but some are unwanted, and UTI tops the list. I hope I'll live to be in my 90's, a world traveler who is uniquely me, as long as my mind is sound and my urinary tract clear. Strange set of priorities? Maybe, but get to that age and tell me you don't understand!

What's a five-letter word for dismayed? It may spell the end for an underwhelmingly, unfortunate, underachieving me, though friends say none of those "U" words accurately describe me and that I am undeniably more. So, I will embrace all that makes me unique while my mind, body, and spirit are still in uniform, and will I will remember to honor the unicorn that is in all of us.

"V" is for Vision

I was hit with some "Oh my gosh, I am old" moments this month. There is a small comfort in knowing I am in good company.

I was talking with someone about watching fireworks as part of the Fourth of July celebration. I volunteered to work the last shift of the evening, selling beer and wine tickets, and asked my friend to join me. The shift ended when the fireworks were set to go off—around 9:30 that evening.

"9:30? That's so late," she complained.

"Yeah, but they do have to wait for it to get dark," I explained.

"I hate driving after dark. I can't see anymore," she said.

And with that, I shut up because I have also become "one of those people". Suddenly, I can't see after dark, suffering as does the proverbial bat and the lessor-known rhinos and gorillas. Gorillas not being able to see after dark makes sense, being so close to us, genetically speaking, but gorillas also sleep 12 hours each night so it's not much of a factor for them.

Rhinos don't see well in the daylight, and bats, well bats made not seeing at night famous – they have adapted with an incredible sense of hearing – humans, not so much. Of course, none of them are trying to navigate a vehicle after sundown.

Our evolutionary adaptation is lagging.

When I was a teenager, pre-driving age, I would beg my parents -- my mother anyway -- for a ride home or to occasionally be the driver of my friends when we planned an activity, but more often than not, me getting permission to go anywhere required working out transportation that did not involve her.

She was in her 50's by then and I never really questioned her refusal to help as anything less than lazy, but now think it likely that poor vision may have played a factor in the "figure it out" stance. Sure, she was probably also exhausted, but not being able to see well would certainly be a deterrent.

I used to love to drive at night. Less traffic, higher rates of speed for road trips. Now I find myself hemming and hawing over social invitations that are taking place too far from home that might keep me out past dusk. It's not my lack of energy; it's my lack of sight. I wear contacts and they are useless when it comes to driving after the sun goes down. I have gotten into the habit of carrying a storage case and solution along with a pair of glasses in my car, lest I find myself needing to drive after sunset and even then, the trip can be iffy.

Recently I was asked to pick a friend up from the airport at ten o'clock PM. The airport is about sixty-five miles away, twenty-five of those miles on a two-lane highway to the interstate. I've driven the route a thousand times, but even with my trusty spectacles on my face, I found myself squinting my way down the familiar roadway, cleaning the lenses while at a red light, running the windshield cleaner a few times, questioning my ability, looking away from the glare of oncoming vehicles, thankful for a lonely stretch of road where the high beams were my friend.

It occurred to me that while my night vision is certainly poor, it's more about my lack of confidence in my ability and my belief that I'm losing that ability that plays a part, because then this happened: I picked up my pal and began taking the same route home (but in reverse) with no difficulty whatsoever. We began to talk and continued nonstop about her travels and our lives and before it really registered, we were 50 miles closer to home—without any issues over oncoming headlights or coming perilously close to cement highway dividers when passing the 18 wheelers (intimidating). My attention was only partially on the road. I was deep in conversation, and I was just fine. A bit of mind over matter, and in that case, at least partially, mind does matter. Driving alone, I had psyched myself into thinking I was no longer up to the task of night driving, but with just enough distraction that comes with conversation, I went on autopilot and drove as I had been doing for decades.

There is a medical explanation for the lack of clarity after dark – our pupils shrink with age, so less light gets in, which is essential for night driving. There is also the likelihood of developing cataracts which affect contrast, glaucoma which narrows your field of vision day or night, Vitamin A deficiency and my personal favorite, FUCH's dystrophy which may result in a sensitivity to glare, to which I say, "FUCH that"!

A solution may be found with my optometrist and a prescription for night driving glasses, an up-to-date examination, an eye lift or maybe in this age of modern conveniences, it's time to call it and try a ride share!

This is certainly not the life I had envisioned. A good

part of my retirement dream includes travel and some of that travel will mean driving across strange landscapes on "dark desert highways."

At any rate, the appeal of a matinee and an early bird special is becoming increasingly clear. While I have not yet fallen into early naps and refusing to leave the house after dark, I do see myself slowing down. Time and distance are now factors to consider before accepting invitations or deciding on destinations. I had not considered vision to be the driving force for these early evenings in, but that may have been short sighted. We will have to wait and see how it all plays out.

"W" is for Weary

I am weary. Something happened the day this body hit 60. I think the warranty expired on all parts and things just started to fail me—my back, ankles, knees, any tightness in my skin, wrinkles, parts of my upper arm just hanging there, resting at the elbow.

I rarely get sick, but now when I do, it becomes an "all hands-on deck" adventure. My achy body and cold-like symptoms often progress to bronchitis, and instead of a few days, it is a few weeks before I recover. Being sick is exhausting, as I work twice as hard to complete the simplest of tasks.

I'm weary indeed, but I am trying to focus on the wonderful parts of growing older and am incredibly grateful for the wisdom that comes with age. I try to focus on all the wonder in the world—sun rises and sunsets, babies, that sort of miraculous, in-your-face, wonder! I love being at the beach watching endless waves crash to the shore. I do still feel small there.

What has 60 plus years of living taught me that is worth sharing? It's mind boggling to me that I'm in this age group, knowing my life is, likely, at least two-thirds played out.

I've learned to let go of the little things, to value time and experiences with loved ones over material goods. I've learned sometimes just staying in place is the only thing to do.

And while I have learned to accept many things, I have

still not come to terms with my body image and my issues around weight. I want to be over, weight. I am not saying I want to be overweight. I denounce the number my scale reveals loud and clear. No, I want to be 'over' weight. I have been, in some form, trying to lose weight in earnest since 1989.

More than three decades ago, I first put money down in the hopes of gaining control over my weight.

I signed up for one of those prepackaged food programs with counseling groups and successfully dropped about 25 pounds. I then got pregnant and gained 55. The baby was under 9 pounds, and that left me with a lot of work to do!

Over the years I have tried just about everything there is— points, shakes, pills, plans, hypnosis, therapy, bets, clubs, books, and meetings—and met varying degrees of short-lived success. I often tell people I have lost about 300 pounds over the last 25 years, but I have gained about 350.

Today my goal weight is the number the scale read back in 1989 that prompted me to seek professional help!

Could I please be as fat as I was the first time I thought I was fat? Self-talk and self-loathing must come to a stop, which makes me think about body image.

Obviously, the media has a high hand in shaping (excuse the pun) my view. The concept of what the ideal woman looks like in Hollywood is just not reality based. At a certain point, intellectually, I know this. We all do.

However, from our earliest memories of Barbie to every fashion magazine and every form of media, thin is in and anything else is less than. Of course thin is in, until you are too thin.

Hollywood ideals is skewed.

Examine country singer Wynonna Judd. For years I watched Wynonna next to her mom on stage, saw her Oprah interviews, including a series on OWN, and I have always thought she must be a behemoth.

The woman towered over her mother and was at least twice her size. I thought she must be big boned. So, imagine my surprise when through some good fortune, I had the opportunity to meet Miss Judd and it turned out that she is only about 5 feet, 5 inches tall and our bones are about the same size. I was shocked to see how average she is! Her mother and her sister must be teeny tiny.

How can we possibly compare ourselves to the size 0 stars we see on television? But compare I do. I am concerned about the example I have given to my children, especially my daughter. For as long as she can remember, I have been trying to lose weight. And while I worked diligently to make sure I did not body shame her and tried to keep her from having a skewed vision of what her body should look like, all she has ever known is my never-ending quest for a thinner me and my failure in achieving it.

Her body issues come from that vantage point. She may not even bother to try to be fit. And for that I worry.

My husband has developed a system that works for him. Yes, it includes regular exercise, but he also tracks every calorie. I watched him lose some 40 pounds after we first got married and he made it look so easy. But in truth, it came at a cost and that cost is time and attention. He spends hours and hours maintaining fitness. I am not convinced the cost/benefit ratio really makes sense, but it's become an integral part of his lifestyle.

I outweigh him by about 50 pounds, and I hold it against him! Luckily, he doesn't hold it against me. He loves me regardless. He just wants me to be healthy. So, I bit the bullet and made fitness part of my lifestyle too.

I work out regularly. I have not lost weight. I have had to come to terms with the fact that being fit and being fat are not mutually exclusive.

What I realize is the number on the scale is not what is important. Being fit and healthy is what matters, and a good diet and regular exercise are necessary to ensure that. I have learned you cannot out-exercise a poor diet and you cannot "bank" fitness. My struggle to get to a certain number continues.

Diets have proven to be temporary and the aftermath more damaging, so I have resisted trying yet another food plan. My body image is without a doubt the biggest frustration of my life. I will continue my journey to be "over" weight, which includes accepting myself and living my life. It means accepting the packaging and focusing on the contents.

But again, I am weary. Tired of the battle. Resistant to the resistance that is my slowing metabolism.

And I am wary of the latest trends toward thinness. I will confess to trying the diabetes related drugs that have a weight loss benefit. They worked great until my insurance stopped covering the medication and the cost without insurance was prohibitive for the tax bracket in which I live. Faster than I could imagine, the pounds began to pile back on, and all my old diet tricks failed. Could it be metabolism?

The wisdom that comes with all these years of living tells

me that the shape of my vessel is not what matters. But the body shame runs deep. I was thinking that being plump used to be a sign of wealth – until food and inexpensive, fast food became readily available and before we knew it, thin became the marker of high society. My theory is that once the drugs proven to help people lose weight become accessible to people of all economies, fat will be back!

Really, I just want to quit and see how round I would be if I just let myself go. For once, I would be ahead of the curve!

Unfortunately, the alternative of just letting myself fall apart does not seem like a wise option, so I will continue to work out faithfully, accept new challenges and pay attention to what I am eating. In the process, I hope to find myself happy with who I am no matter what size that happens to be, and I can put the weight issue to rest.

Hollie Grimaldi-Flores

"X" is for Xerosis

It would have been too easy to go with x-ray for this letter. Who has made it to old age without one? But no, my thoughts are on my skin. The crepe thin parts, the brown spotted parts, the wrinkled parts, the hanging down parts and the dry parts. Xerosis is the medical name for dry skin. It comes from Greek: 'xero' means 'dry' as in "there is xero moisture left in your skin!"

A lack of moisture in the skin, which may be the result of aging, is rudely referred to as senile Xerosis. Sometimes it can be a sign of an underlying disease such as diabetes.

At any rate, it boils down to that dry, rough, scaly, flaky skin I work hard to keep soft and moist each day. I have been blessed with soft skin. I have had it called out many times, from boyfriends to girlfriends, even my children have remarked on the softness of my skin. I cannot take any credit for the natural state of my epidermis.

But even the softest skin can become dry and scaly if neglected. One indelible memory I have of my mother is noticing one day how incredibly flaky and white the skin on her legs were. She was not one for self-care and it showed up on her skin. She may as well have been part lizard. That woman could shed some skin!

I don't think I had hit my teen years yet, but even then, I knew she was simply in need of some body moisturizer. I vowed right then and there that I would never let my legs get so dry that the skin flaked! To this day, my legs are the first part of my body to get coated in lotion after I towel dry.

Fast forward a half a century, and as with so many aspects in life, I realize, I owe my mom yet another apology. I had no idea how her life was going or that her dry skin was merely a symptom. The woman simply did not prioritize taking care of herself because there we so many others to whom she gave care. She was likely overwhelmed most of the years I was growing up, as the youngest of her seven children. She passed on her naturally healthy skin but also her lack of self-care and I still struggle to take the time and expense of properly carrying for this vessel. While I refuse to let my skin become dry to the point of lizard like appearance, I do tend to lean toward the most economical (read: cheapest) lotions on the market.

Keeping up appearances is consuming and expensive! I shudder to think of the countless hours as teenagers, my girlfriends and I would spend looking through magazines, trying on clothes, experimenting with makeup and hair and of course, staring in the mirror. There's a reason they call it a vanity! Of course, none of it is bad if explored for its own value, but I look back with judgment because the entirety of our focus was our quest to be appealing to the opposite sex.

We were not thinking of how beneficial our primping and polishing would be as we aged. No, we just wanted to be noticed by the boys we had crushes on at school.

One of the nice things about being the age I am now is that the need to keep up my appearance to attract a mate is long past. There is confidence that comes with not needing to look a certain way in the quest to attract a romantic partner. Some might say maintenance must be done to keep the mate I found, but at this stage in the game, I have nothing more to prove.

That fact became very clear a few years ago when I spent a weekend visiting one of my dearest girlfriends. She was finishing up treatment for breast cancer and I decided to visit her in celebration. Because she had a teenager and husband at home, we booked a room at a resort not too far from her house and pretended we were both on vacation.

We were lounging at the hotel pool when a large group of twenty-somethings showed up, along with a DJ and a portable bar. It turned out that our hotel was also close to a ballpark hosting spring training for some major league teams, and a group staying there thought our little oasis would be the perfect spot for a little aquatic tailgating.

Soon, along with the plethora of young men, came a gaggle of girls wandering around in short skirts and skimpy tops, teetering on three-inch stilettos. There was a lot of drinking and posing and my friend and I remarked more than once how happy we were to have passed through that era of insecurity and endless searching. Sure, they were young and beautiful, but we both could see the likelihood of heartbreak and disappointment oozing from the scene. The young men flexing their muscles and cashing in on hours spent in the gym.; the young gals parading past in a dazzling display of hair, makeup and wardrobe as if the cement pool was a Hollywood movie set.

"I kind of miss being that young, but I think I prefer this vantage point," I said to my friend. What a sight we must have been as we sat there splayed out on our lounge chairs in our hotel-supplied bathrobes, finishing off the last slices of a pie we had brought to the pool!

I can imagine one of the malnourished lasses noticing the two of us and praying they would never be that old, but honestly, no one in that group was checking out the two older ladies eating dessert in their bathrobes at the pool! Something incomprehensible just a few decades prior. I do appreciate the freedom in that. Even if they did have some pointed comments to say, we could take it: we have thick skin!

We were covered from head to toe, protecting ourselves from the damaging sun. Our skin had already endured decades of over exposure in pursuit of a darker hue. As young girls, we would lay on black pavement with aluminum foil under our heads, lemon juice in our hair and vegetable oil on our skin. I don't know what the SPF rating is for Crisco, but I imagine it is a negative number.

At this point in our lives, our skin has been stretched beyond recognition as we gestated babies. Our skin has soaked up gallons of lotions with and without UV protection. Our skin has been poked and prodded and broken open more than once. It's been burned and peeled. It has been exfoliated, shaved, plucked, and tweezed. For some it has been nipped and tucked and cut and lifted. And that's all just to speak of what we do to it of our own volition! Our faces have become more akin to road maps than smooth canvas. It took decades to get us to cover our heads with a brimmed hat and protect our eyes with proper sunglasses that were more than a fashion statement.

Our lives have unfolded, and our priorities have changed. Sure, we take care to stay healthy and are more cautious than we could have ever convinced our younger selves to be. We know we are heading toward our final days. And today, the dryest parts of our bodies are no longer on the surface, if you get my meaning!

I am glad we can laugh at those younger selves and are living more authentically.

Whenever death comes for me, I plan to have a smile, and plenty of moisturizer, on this wrinkled, saggy, baggy sack of skin, and if I have my druthers, I'll be enjoying a plate full of pie.

"Y" is for Youth

My daughter, who is not yet 30, called the other day to tell me she would like to be finished with "adulting." "It's hard," she exclaimed. I agreed.

Life is full of difficulties. Being an adult is not easy. Sometimes, it all feels senseless. The trick is finding something meaningful that makes it all worthwhile. And the old saying rings true: "Youth is wasted on the young." It is no wonder we often look back with a sense of longing.

When I was young, I simply could not wait to be an adult. Truly, I did not wait. I hurried through the growing-up years as quickly as possible.

As the youngest child, it was natural for me to want to emulate my older siblings. It seems I was always in a rush to grow up. I did not let anything get in the way of my independence.

In elementary school, I made arrangements for a ride home because I wanted to be able to participate in activities taking place after the last bell rang. My parents driving me home at that time was not a possibility and they did not offer a solution. I got creative and found a school employee who had to drive right by the end of my road when their workday was over, which coincided with the end of practice. Issue resolved. I was nine.

As soon as I did not need a babysitter for myself, I began earning my own money. Watching other people's children was never my favorite chore so as soon as I was old enough, I got a job. I delivered the morning edition of the local newspaper at age 14. Later, I was hired at the local fruit stand as a cashier. During my last year of high school, I added a work-study job to my morning. Two jobs helped me afford my share of the rent of the apartment I shared with a girlfriend during the last half of my senior year.

I think it is fair to say I was in a bit of a rush to "adult." In my youth I was a fearless, reckless, unpredictable woman in motion. It is worth repeating that I abused my body with considerable portions of alcohol, drugs, cheap fuel, and poor decisions, but recovery was quick, and any self-inflicted pain passed quickly. I thought myself to be bulletproof.

I know I had plenty of elders telling me to slow down, but I could not hear them. I wanted all the freedom I believed came with being an adult. I could not see the bondage. It was impossible to know then that those would be some of the easiest days of my life.

So, of course I tried to spare my children from rushing to adulthood. The world moved faster and the exposure to so much of everything came so much quicker than it did for me—even on my accelerated plan. I delayed the "Santa Claus conversation" for as long as possible. I made their lunches well into their years in high school. I coddled. I protected. But I also gave gentle nudges toward independence. I hope they think of their time as children fondly, but adulthood was the next stop. And, as a parent, it was the job—to give them a base from which to spread their wings and stand back as they took flight. I admit to hovering with my mommy net, occasionally offering a soft place to land.

My challenge has always been to step back and let them find their own way. I had to learn (and am still learning) to allow them to make mistakes, experience setbacks, and find the fortitude to forge ahead.

The parenting job can be excruciating.

When I look back on my early days of adulting, I see someone who was determined and creative and brave. (It is also possible the word, naïve comes into play.) I can see the same characteristics in them.

So far, they have not made any choices that limit their options moving forward.

I see my kids living their lives. They make false starts. They struggle. They sometimes fail.

More often, they succeed, and they have only just begun.

I think I, too, have had enough of adulting for now. What if I took a pass on adulthood for just a while? Let someone else run the rat race? I could spend my days lying in the grass watching clouds float by. I could call up my friends and go for a hike by the river. We could spend hours watching movies or reading novels. We could get the other folks on the street together for a game of tag or hide and seek.

I would spend hours in classrooms soaking up every morsel of knowledge my teachers were trying to impart. It would be super helpful to be able to identify foreign countries on a map, and to be just a bit more comfortable discussing recent history. I would take more classes in the arts.

Learning the periodic table might become a useful tool, and in today's world, mastering a second or third language would be so beneficial!

However, any sort of math after algebra would still be avoided at all costs!

I would spend more time in creative endeavors and not be so quick to give up on anything I found remotely difficult to master.

Maybe it is true, what I have heard—it's never too late to have a happy childhood!

I have been a certified adult for quite a while now. It does come with a lot of freedom, mostly of choice, and it comes with a great deal of responsibility.

I know my grown-up children will find their stride and thrive in this new perspective life has to offer them.

The bulk of their story is still unfolding. I can hardly wait to see how it all turns out.

"Z" is for Zig Zag

As I look back on the life I have lived, thus far, I clearly see there are turning point decisions, times when I zigged but should have zagged. Decisions that seemingly changed the path I had been on. I sometimes wonder if I would have ended up in the same place regardless of those decisions, the whole predestined versus free will debate. But no amount of "what if'ing" changes the past. And so, I embrace the younger version of me and the choices she made.

Each of the decades of my life has made me a little stronger mentally and emotionally, a little wiser and incredibly grateful to still be on the journey.

I had lunch, recently, with a friend who is in her early 80's and she is remarkable, as are so many other people I know who are in their "golden years". Seventy used to seem so old. Eighty, ancient! Not so much, anymore.

But a shift does happen. My eighty-something-year-old friend said she loved the time she was my age. She was still going and doing and being without a care. She mentioned that she has a lot more fear now—fear of falling, fear of breaking something, fear of driving, fear of crowds, fear of illness. I agreed that as I have gotten older, I have noticed an increase in fear also.

Things I never would have thought twice about now give me pause.

How ironic that as we get closer to the end of our time

here, with more years behind us than in front of us, we become more fearful, yet when we are just starting our lives, with so much more to lose, we are fearless! Quite a paradox.

Some might say we grow wiser, meaning being more practical and more aware, but I think, generally speaking, we lose our willingness to take risks. What a shame. We learn from our mistakes to the point that we stop trying. I'm not talking about being reckless, but our overall sense of adventure seems to diminish with each passing decade. We become more set in our ways. We become more sedentary. We become less social. We spend more time reminiscing than we do creating new memories. Our world is becoming smaller.

But if we are lucky, the memories are good and plentiful.

At a recent birthday celebration, one of my kids asked me what my favorite decade has been so far. It's a tough question.

I thought again about how I spent my childhood wishing I was grown, so while I had a lot of fun in those carefree days of adolescence and into my teens, I would not say those decades ranked very high on the list. Best in some ways, not so great in others.

My twenties were filled with major life changes—college, moving across the country, getting married and having my first child. Some big stuff took place in that decade, but I can't say it was my best.

In my thirties, I became clearer about the kind of person I was and the life I wanted to live. I had a second child and a divorce and a ton of therapy! These were good years, but there were some really hard times as well.

There are many variables to consider when deciding which would be the best span, but overall, my forties were probably the most enjoyable. It was a busy decade. I remarried and suddenly my little family of three became a party of nine. I was working in broadcasting and loved it and was heavily involved in my community. It was a busy time and culminated with most of the offspring growing up and living on their own. My social life was very busy. My work life was gratifying. My home life was hectic.

Looking back, it was the best of times!

In my fifties I had to make the adjustment from the day-to-day responsibilities of parenting children to the infrequent call to parent adults. With the kids grown, there was a shift back to couple-ness with my spouse. I tried to find my way back from being a mother, to being the person I once was, and realized that girl was long gone! I had to reinvent myself. I took a risk on a career change and redefined who I was as a person. My physical self-made some harrowing changes. Life got a little easier and a little less busy. That may have been my best decade, if not for the woes of this aging body.

Now here I am in the early years of this next decade with much more freedom. While parenting never truly ends, the bulk of that job is finished. My husband and I are finally able to make plans that are just about us. There is time to relax and to begin thinking about what retirement will look like. There is time to explore the planet. But even as I write this, I am also acutely aware that my body continues its own steady march, and not into battle, unless that battle is downhill! This decade has the potential to be the best decade yet, but again, it's the physical part of the journey that seems to be taking a toll, putting a damper on qualifying as the best.

As you must surely know by now, my husband does battle with age every day. He has a consistent workout regimen. He is disciplined and committed to taking care of his physical self and still his body rebels. It seems futile. But to quote Clint Eastwood, he "refuses to let the old man in."

Since I am not as disciplined or committed to taking care of my physical self, it would make perfect sense that my body would fail me, so I should really take advantage of each day! It is only a matter of time, literally.

When I get there, I hope to be as vibrant as my 80-something-year-old friend.

I think the key is maintaining good friendships, a robust social life, having purpose, living with a grateful heart and hopefully, a strong body that will keep up with my spirit.

Each decade has had its good and its bad points. As I age, I hope that despite the aches and pains, I remain grateful for the privilege of getting old.

A great number of my physical features have seemed to call it quits, from my eye lids to my ankles, many of the components of this body really aren't even trying anymore!

Sure, there were plenty of times when I zigged and should have zagged, but it all added up to me sitting here today and sharing these thoughts with you.

Who knows, the best may be yet to come!

They Aren't Even Trying Anymore

Acknowledgements

My heartfelt appreciation to my first readers, Marci Zampi, for her editing skill and her guidance in keeping each essay from being too redundant, and to my first born, Tea Wade, for their suggestions and contributions and for continually helping me be a better person; to my husband Ernie Flores for being unconditionally supportive; to the Flores boys and my family of origin, for vast amounts of material; and to my daughter, Courtney Wade, for reminding me to be brave.

Love and gratitude to my posse of women on both coasts, who listen to and support me when I am at my highest highs and lowest lows, including Shanin Martin, Barbara DeHart, Denise Johnson, Lisa Swarthout, Nancy Taylor, Joni Enders, Lynn Walsh, Cathy Williams, Michelle Smith, Karen Durfee and Erin Kate Hooper. If I forgot someone, know it is simply fatigue.

Thank you to Dr. Max Vogt, the person I credit with convincing me that I could and should write a book, (albeit over 20 years ago), and for writing my first review, which comprises, in part, the back cover of this book.

This book would not have happened without the assistance and guidance of Jan Fishler. Thank you for your counsel, friendship, and example.

And to my book club ladies, I have a suggestion for next month's read!

Hollie Grimaldi-Flores

About the Author

Hollie was born and raised in central New York, the youngest of seven children. She moved to California in 1985, living in the San Francisco Bay Area, Marin and Sonoma Counties before moving to Nevada County in 1995.

In 2001 she married Ernie Flores and together they raised a blended family of five boys, one nonbinary person and a girl, now all adults.

Hollie spent 20 years in the media industry, as an award-winning on-air radio talent, and later as a columnist and contributor for her local newspaper.

She continues to actively volunteer and sits on boards and commissions in her community.

Contact her at www.HollieGrimaldi.com and sure to listen to her podcast, "HollieGrams", available on most streaming services.